the **calendar girls** story

the calendar girls story

by **Jim Simpson** and the real Calendar Girls

Dalesman

First published in Great Britain 2004 by
Dalesman Publishing Company Limited
Stable Courtyard, Broughton Hall
Skipton, North Yorkshire, BD23 3AZ
www.dalesman.co.uk

Text © Dalesman Publishing Co Ltd 2004
Unless stated otherwise, photographs © Buena Vista International
(UK) Ltd 2004

A British Library Cataloguing-in-Publication record
is available for this book.

ISBN 1 85568 211 7

Colour origination by Grasmere Digital Imaging Limited
Design, layout, printing and binding by Butler & Tanner Ltd

All royalties from the sale of this book are being donated
to the Leukaemia Research Fund.

LEUKAEMIA RESEARCH
HODGKIN'S | LYMPHOMA | MYELOMA

registered charity 216032

contents

 # foreword

The true story of the Calendar Girls which inspired the film is about so much more than just some women shocking the world with a risqué calendar.

When the tale first broke in the press I – like everyone else – thought how hilarious it all was: so very English, funny and wickedly mischievous. It certainly upset a lot of notions about what the Women's Institute got up to.

But there is so much more involved in this story, both in real life and in the film. It touches on the larger issues of life. It is about bereavement and friendship, about losing your sense of self and then being able to regain it. The women's experiences also show the importance of a strong community and how this can help the people in it – and that is something that a lot of places have lost in our modern society.

The landscape of the Dales is an important element in the story too. Although I had been there many years ago I had not realised how very different it is to the rest of Britain nor how stunningly rugged and deeply romantic it is.

There is, for me, a very personal link with both the story itself and the purpose of the film and this book. John Baker died because of a lymphoma and my own daughter, Maisie, suffered leukaemia. Maisie – now sixteen – recovered and I know the importance of the work of the Leukaemia Research Fund, which is supported by the royalties from both the film and this book.

Julie Walters

Angela Baker and Julie Walters

beginnings

'The night my dad died, my mum went into the nurses' room and told them "We'll be back. You've not heard the last of us. I won't say any more, but we will do something".' Matthew Baker

On a September's night in London's Leicester Square, a succession of limousines have lined up to deliver well-known names and faces to the red carpet outside Europe's largest cinema. To one side of the carpet, television crews and reporters jostle to get comment from the stars, while photographers shout out names to get their prey's attention for a swift snap that will fill the next day's newspapers. On the other side, a temporary grandstand has been erected for the public to get their own view of the stars.

But treading through this gauntlet are not just the actors, the television stars and players of the film industry, for among these were the ordinary people who actually made this possible: the Calendar Girls. A radiographer, a registrar, a dress-shop owner, a headmaster's wife, an artist and a college administrator are all being honoured for their extraordinary story, the basis for the film. After all the celebrities have given their two-minute soundbites to the media and made their

way through the doors of the cinema, there is a pause. The six women link arms and march, united, up the red carpet as the crowd rises to a standing ovation.

In the course of four years their bold idea, a risqué calendar offering an alternative view of the

At the première in Leicester Square, (*Left to right*) Angela Baker, Tricia Stewart, Chris Clancy, Terry Logan, Ros Fawcett, Lynda Logan and Beryl Bamforth.

traditional country pursuits of the Women's Institute, has taken them all around the world. But it is all rooted in their homes in North Yorkshire. As Nick Barton, one of the film's producers, notes: 'I don't think that if they had been in, say, Surrey Women's Institute or Suffolk or Sussex, that the calendar would have been made.'

All the women have met through living in Cracoe. It is not the prettiest village in the Dales, though it has the area's trademark drystone walls snaking up the steep fells that overlook its stone-built houses and cottages. In effect, the village is a single street through which traffic hurtles on its way to either the massive quarry a few miles further along the

Main Street, Cracoe.

road or to the far prettier hamlets that nestle on the banks of the River Wharfe. The observant eye might note a pub, a café and a farm shop, but most people pass through without a second glance, intent on reaching the quaint market towns, the matchless views and imposing fells that lie further up the dale.

'we're parochial, in the sense that we care about the community, because if we don't care, who else is going to?' *Beryl Bamforth*

But it is Cracoe, not the far more picturesque fictional village of Knapeley, that produced the story that inspired *Calendar Girls*, the film. The village has changed its character over the past thirty years and is no longer the place where workers for the local farms and estates live. Its people are now more likely to be in business or are professionals working in the cities of Leeds or Bradford. But the tale of the ladies who stripped off for a charity calendar, and the thousands upon thousands of pounds that they have raised, is rooted in the old values and virtues of village life.

Beryl Bamforth, the most senior figure among the women featured in the original calendar, puts it this way:

'I feel we're parochial, in the sense that we care about the community, because if we don't care, who else is going to?'

This sense of community is shared among the 200 or so people who make up the village, so that

Kettlewell (*right*), location for the fictitious town of Knapeley in *Calendar Girls*.

everybody knows everybody else and, more significantly, there are strong bonds between them. These friendships are reinforced by shared activities including, of course, the Women's Institute to which nearly all the women involved in producing the calendar belonged and which spawned the idea in the first place.

'I just turned to Angela and said "We should do our own calendar. An alternative to Pirelli with crafts", and she just laughed.' *Tricia Stewart*

Tricia Stewart, or 'Trish' to her friends, explains: 'Every year, each area of the WI produces a traditional calendar with bridges, churches or landscapes, and every year we are asked if we have photographs to submit. But this particular year at the meeting, I just turned to Angela and said "We should do our own calendar. An alternative to Pirelli with crafts", and she just laughed. Over supper we talked about the idea to a few other girls, but it was a joke and we never really thought it would happen.'

And so the idea was kicking around in various forms for some time before it became a reality. Lynda Logan recalls an earlier version: 'Before that, Trish had suggested to me that I should do a painting of her and some friends in the nude. She said that, when we were really old, we would be able to have a painting showing that we didn't look that bad in our forties and fifties. I encouraged her because I thought it was a funny idea, not because I thought it would turn out as it has. It was just because of the devilment in me.'

Angela Baker says they even got to the stage of

Tricia Stewart, the inspiration for Chris in the film, and the originator of the idea for the calendar.

Chris and Annie (Helen Mirren and Julie Walters) greet the prospect of a new WI calendar with unbridled enthusiasm.

Ros Fawcett ran the local café.

planning how they would stage the painting. 'Trish thought that we could go into the woods somewhere and Lynda would place us round the trees. We'd have bin liners, we thought, and then we'd drop these bin liners and Lynda would paint us.'

Nor was it just the women who were in on the act. It was a joke held in common with all. Terry Fletcher, a journalist who took part in Tricia's Friday night yoga session, knew about the nude calendar idea and thought nothing of it. He says:

'During one of these sessions, Tricia said that perhaps they ought to do a nude calendar, which everybody took as being one of her madcap ideas, of which there were three every half hour, but I didn't take much notice. She asked that if they did a nude calendar, could I get them into the papers, knowing I was a journalist, and I remember saying, "Trish, if you did a nude calendar I couldn't keep you out of the papers". Everybody laughed and forgot all about it, until probably eighteen months later.'

The calendar was only possible because of the deep bonds between the women, who between

'I was a bit choosy. I'd wait until there was a good speaker and then get someone to invite me. I also got involved in the concerts that Beryl organised.'   Ros Fawcett

them have racked up decades of friendship, and the rest of the village. The Women's Institute is one vital connection between all the girls involved. All were members, except Ros Fawcett, who ran the local café for many years. She explains:

'I wasn't a member of the WI because Rylstone and District WI were renowned for their wonderful suppers, and the last thing I wanted to do after being in a café all day was take my turn at doing suppers. So I was a bit choosy. I'd wait until there was a good speaker and then get someone to invite me. I also got involved in the concerts that Beryl organised.'

For the others, the WI was one of the village traditions, the way in which everyone was introduced to everybody else. As Angela Baker puts it:

'A lady knocked on the door and invited me. I didn't even know what it stood for. I'd never heard of it. She explained that they meet once a month and it's just a way of getting to know people.'

Beryl Bamforth says that the local WI was one of the first things she sought out when she and her husband Terry moved into the village from South Yorkshire in the 1960s, when he took over the headship of the tiny village school. The popularity of the WI and the loyalty it inspired also meant that many remained members even if they moved out of the village, as Christine Clancy did.

Other village activities also bound the group together. For instance, Beryl was heavily involved in amateur dramatics, the Grassington Players, while her husband conducted the Hetton and Rylstone Choir. This involved other members of the village in turn, so Angela and John Baker were both involved in the choir, John in particular being remembered as an 'excellent tenor'. The pub quiz on a Monday night was another popular occasion that got the villagers mixing with one another.

Tricia's Friday night yoga class at Cracoe Memorial Hall, known locally as 'the Hut', was

Beryl Bamforth (*third from left*) with Angela, Tricia and Ros during the filming of *Calendar Girls*.

another activity that brought many like-minded villagers together. Angela recalls: 'We used to look forward to it because all the cares of the week used to just fade away. It was brilliant. It was a mixed group because the men loved it too.' And Tricia quips: 'What with the WI and yoga, if you weren't doing the Cat (a yoga position) you'd be baking a cake for the next meeting.'

Tricia would take her class through the Hatha yoga she had learnt over five years, together with exercises drawn from other disciplines such as Pilates and the Alexander Technique. This would build up from gentle stretches to more demanding exercises aimed at improving posture and flexibility. The evening would always end with a total relaxation, after winding down through either breathing with alternate nostrils or chanting the Vedic mantra 'Aum'. She says:

'The hut was lovely. The windows used to rattle when the wagons went past during relaxation, but

The new village Hall at Cracoe, which replaced 'the Hut' where Tricia held her yoga classes.

Tricia's Friday night yoga classes in Cracoe Memorial Hall were translated into hilltop t'ai chi sessions in the film.

it had such charm. Then they took the curtains out because it was a fire risk but I took candles in. I shouldn't have as it was a fire hazard, but without them there would be no atmosphere. John [Baker] never used to do the build-up to relaxation, he'd just go to sleep.' But, once relaxed, Tricia would then read poems or some words she found especially wise and John, she says, 'always told me to read slowly'.

If the WI and yoga were a mainstay of the village social life, the everyday work and daily rhythms of the community also made for close ties, as Ros Fawcett points out: 'I met Angela first through her son Matthew, who was at Cracoe School. In 1981, he knocked on my door at the café and asked me to sponsor him for a sweet suck. He was dressed in lederhosen and a bonny young lad, very polite. We'd just moved into the café and were absolutely

skint. I said "Yes, I'll sponsor you for £1 a minute". And he came back saying "You owe me £19". He'd sucked it for nineteen minutes. That made us laugh. I also started doing hairdressing round the village and got to meet Angela. Tricia came into the café on the day she moved in with her children, and we've known them ever since.'

Tricia remembers Angela as one of the first neighbours to introduce herself when the family moved to Cracoe and the one who recruited her into the WI.

'I was only thirty-five, so I told her it wasn't at the top of my list of priorities, but she said it would look odd if I didn't join,' she recollects.

The three women, Ros, Tricia and Angela, also developed a daily routine that drew them closer, a morning walk with their dogs up the fell that over-looks Cracoe. It started around seven o'clock,

Angela, Ros and Tricia on a recent walk up to the Sheep Pens.

when Angela and Tricia would meet and then walk down to the corner of the road that led up the hill to the Sheep Pens, the place where the local farmer would gather sheep from the fell. The dogs would then be ignored as the women walked and talked their way to the top of the steep hill, where they would perform a couple of complete yoga breaths followed by a Pilates exercise for the neck and shoulders called the Corkscrew. Then they would make their way back to the village, discussing everything from diets to husbands.

'It's a very positive way to start the day,' says Tricia. 'Then I would have breakfast with John and Angela, because he got into the habit of making breakfast for three while we were out walking.'

And, as all had children of roughly similar ages, naturally they grew up together, went to school together and played out together. Then, Lynda and

'I would have breakfast with John and Angela, because he got into the habit of making breakfast for three while we were out walking.'

Tricia Stewart

Terry Logan moved to the village and became the Bakers' next-door neighbours. Both are artists. Terry works in watercolours and pastels, while Lynda uses oils, at one point painting Tricia's daughter Lizzi. To mesh the group even more tightly together, Angela's son Matthew married Lynda and Terry's daughter Georgina.

The result was that the women of Cracoe had formed a cohesive and close community that spanned several decades of friendship, unusual in today's world. The Bakers, for instance, first moved into the village in the mid-1970s from Northallerton when John became assistant national park officer for the Yorkshire Dales. So, when he was diagnosed as suffering from cancer in February 1998, it hit everybody, not just his family.

Ros recalls the shock. 'He was a fit, handsome man who glowed with health. That New Year we'd had such fun. We went to some friends for a dinner party, and he liked to sit next to me because I'd let him drink more whisky than Ange would. The next day we all went for a walk on the fell and we

'John was a very fit person who never had time off work and, like everyone, we thought we did the right things.'   *Angela Baker*

John Alderton played John Baker in *Calendar Girls*. He prepared for the role by spending time with the Baker family, going on walks John had enjoyed and, thanks to Angela, wearing John's watch throughout the filming.

thought he was hung over because he lagged behind, but his illness was obviously just starting. Trish was away in Australia when John was diagnosed. Normally Ange would have rung her because they're very close. She rang me, and said that John had to go for tests and she was frightened.'

Angela was completely unprepared, recalling: 'John was a very fit person who never had time off work and, like everyone, we thought we did the right things. We didn't smoke, or drink to excess, walked, spent time outdoors, ate the right things and life was good.'

She first suspected something was wrong when John started to wake up with night sweats. She made a doctor's appointment, thinking it might be just flu. One blood test later and John had an urgent appointment with a surgeon that led to him being booked in for a CT scan, a form of X-ray imaging that provides a three-dimensional picture of the body's internal organs.

'I knew things weren't good when the nurse came and said, "When John comes out, we'll take you to see someone and we'll have a chat". They just said that he had a growth in his small intestine about the size of a large grapefruit, and they thought it was probably malignant, but wouldn't be sure until they removed it and did some tests. He went in for the operation the next day.'

The result was very grim. It was an aggressive form of non-Hodgkin's Lymphoma. A lymphoma is a cancer of the lymphatic system, the lymph glands and channels to be found throughout the body. The lymphatic system collects lymph, the fluid that bathes all body cells, and is an important part of the body's immune system. There are thirty-five types of lymphoma, divided into Hodgkin's and non-Hodgkin's. When fatal, death is caused by the failure of organs invaded by or near the tumour

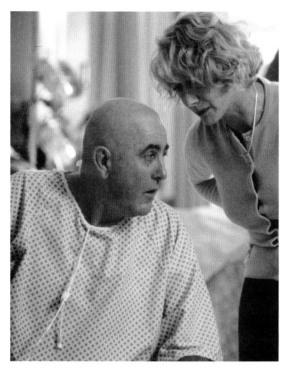

John Baker had to endure four bouts of chemotherapy.

Annie and John share precious time looking out over one of their favourite views.

mass not, as in leukaemia, because of secondary infections or loss of blood.

Angela believes that her husband may have had the tumour for some time because he never really

'They used to just come for support because basically I was scared, although I couldn't tell John this because I had to be really strong.'
                                            Angela Baker

recovered from that operation, even after four bouts of chemotherapy. When he came home from having the treatment, their friends rallied round as best they could to help.

'Ros, Lynda and Trish came and slept on nights when John was at home. They were taking it in turns because it is frightening being on your own when you have someone at home who is very poorly. They used to just come for support because basically I was scared, although I couldn't tell John this because I just had to be really strong.'

Ros explains: 'We just did what we could, really, because they were just so close, so in love and he was such a family man. Angela couldn't bear anybody being sick (she has a phobia about it) so in case John vomited she needed someone there who could clear it up for her.

'He always had a great sense of humour and a great faith. When I went to stay with him overnight, he was very poorly and I think we decided between us he should be back in hospital. But he said he wasn't going anywhere on an empty stomach and he demanded two Weetabix. He was so stubborn. When I walked back into the bedroom, he was

reading a prayer to himself while waiting for the ambulance. I'd never seen anyone with faith like that.'

Meanwhile the Bakers' friends in the village also did what they could. His friends at their Methodist chapel prayed for John, while others sought to raise money to fight the disease. Thirty of them, including Tricia, did a sponsored walk across the famous Three Peaks, the twenty-four-mile route that takes in Yorkshire's highest hills, Whernside, Pen-y-ghent

'It was just one of those magical times that you never forget and he was just laughing.' *Angela Baker*

and Ingleborough, raising £5,000 for the Leukaemia Research Fund, a charity chosen on the advice of John's consultant. Tricia's husband, Ian, opted for a less energetic fundraising option, playing gigs with his band to raise money.

It was at this time that Tricia's idea for an alternative WI calendar resurfaced as a fundraising ploy, at one of the sociable evenings the Bakers were able to enjoy during John's illness.

Angela says: 'We had a brilliant night, when a lot of them came round and John just fancied a pint of beer. We were all chatting, and saying what month we'd like to be and what craft we would do, and how we were going to let John be the token man, because Lynda was going to take the pictures.

Tackling the Three Peaks route.

We thought it would cheer him up. 'It was just one of those magical times that you never forget and he was just laughing. He said we'd never do it, that we were all talk. But at least he knew about it, and that's a really big thing for me.'

Such evenings were a rare relief from the daily routine that now enveloped the Bakers, as Angela took time off from her job as the registrar of births, deaths and marriages in Skipton to tend to her husband. By July, John had been transferred to Leeds General Infirmary, a big teaching hospital where it would be possible to transplant stem cells in an attempt to block the cancer's progress.

'You had to go there with a smile, you know,' says Angela. 'You had to open the door and go "Hi", although you had done nothing since last time except answer the door and the phone because people were constantly asking "How is he?".'

'He would ask: "What news? What have you done?". One day I must not have been able to do it

'[John] potted them up and handed them out to everybody … Everyone seemed to have these little sunflowers growing in their windows.' *Georgina Baker*

and he just said to me: "You look absolutely frightened to death. What's the matter with you?". I said, "Actually, John, it's quite hard to walk into here".'

Matthew Baker and his wife Georgina were also daily visitors. They too found it hard. 'When someone's very, very ill,' they explained, 'you are clutching at straws because there is nothing you can do to help them or say that will make them well again. You can't ask the one question you have: "Are you feeling any better?"'

Georgina says this is how the sunflowers, such a poignant symbol in the calendar, first arose. 'It was the only thing I could think of to help him which might keep him going a bit longer. I noticed all the sunflowers on his get well cards. It was that time of the year for seeding, so I said,"What you should do, John, is pot some sunflower seeds, because when they're out and flowering you should be out and in remission". I went straight to the garden centre in Grassington, bought some sunflower seeds and took them into him.

'He was coming back that weekend, which was very rare, and he potted them up and handed them out to everybody, friends, children down the road, people from the church. Everyone seemed to have these little sunflowers growing in their windows. It was just something that we felt we could do for him.'

As John suffered, so did Angela. She lost two and a half stones, and thought he had not noticed. But in fact he had rung a fellow churchgoer, asking her to look after Angela. Then, after three weeks in the Leeds hospital, John died, the month before the sunflowers blossomed.

Matthew says he knew his mother would do something to mark her husband's death, even if it was not then clear what it would be.

'The night my dad died, my mum said: "We're going to do something". She walked out and went into the nurses' room and told them: "We'll be back. You've not heard the last of us. I won't say any more but we will do something".'

The calendar idea resurfaced about two months later, by which time Angela had changed her job, unable to cope with other people's grief and joy.

'I couldn't keep registering deaths all day. People need someone who is together, not someone who is miserable. And the weddings: I found I

was looking at young couples, thinking "Why us?". It was too hard.'

Instead she opted for a complete change of career, working as an information officer for the Dales National Park in nearby Grassington. One morning, on one of the walks up to the Sheep Pens, Lynda asked Trish: 'Look, are we going to do this calendar? Because, even if we don't sell any, it will give Angela something to do.'

And so they decided to start recruiting their models at the next WI monthly meeting.

Beryl Bamforth, then sixty-five, was one of their first targets. 'Tricia surreptitiously asked me to be a part of the calendar and I thought it would be a bit wimpish to say no, so I accepted. And then went home in horror.' Beryl had then been a member of the WI for thirty-four years, serving as Secretary and as President in her time. She was swiftly joined by five other WI members keen to change the WI's old-fashioned image, and also raise money for a good cause.

Christine Clancy, who worked in administration at nearby Craven College, was another recruit, but recalls being caught unawares in the village pub,

'Tricia came up and said, "We're thinking about doing a nude calendar to raise some money for John. You'll be up for it won't you?". I said, "Oh yes" After having a couple of glasses of wine, it seemed like a good idea'.

Christine Clancy

the Devonshire Arms. 'My husband John and I were in the pub having a drink, and Tricia came up and said "We're thinking about doing a nude calendar to raise some money for John. You'll be up for it, won't you?". I said, "Oh yes". After having a couple of glasses of wine, it seemed like a good idea.'

Once they had assembled most of the models needed for the calendar, Lynda and Tricia decided to hold a brainstorming session in the Devonshire Arms. There they all met to work out which crafts would be represented in what months. Having grown up with *Monty Python's Flying Circus*, with Terry Jones seated nude at a piano, Tricia had always thought of Angela in the same pose, playing *Jerusalem*, the WI anthem, but the others were not quite so easy to imagine. Although by now they had recruited most of their models, they were still missing one, and Ros Fawcett just happened to be in the Devonshire that night with her husband Chris. She had thought that she was safe because she was not a member of the WI, and her first reaction to Tricia's suggestion was 'Gosh no, I'm not stripping off', but this changed when they said it was in memory of John.

'I thought "I can't not be in it". So after a couple of glasses of red wine I went home as Miss November,' says Ros. 'Chris said, "I can't believe you've agreed to be in a nude calendar. You've spent a lifetime going to Weightwatchers and Slimming World, and nothing like that's ever worked for you, so why you want to show off your body now I don't know".'

But now the project had its eleven models and was ready for the next stage: the shoot.

the shoot

'I don't mind admitting that I was terrified. I thought "You must be mad", and I didn't tell a soul until after it was done.'

Christine Clancy

Once the models had been recruited, the question bothering them was: who would be the photographer? Understandably, while some were happy to strip in a good cause, they were concerned about being naked with a man present, even if he was preoccupied with taking the pictures.

Georgina Baker was the first choice, daughter of Terry and Lynda Logan, daughter-in-law of John Baker and an artist herself. But then she was ruled out, as she was having her first child. Another female photographer was then suggested, but she also dropped out. Finally, Lynda was mooted to do the shots, under Terry's direction, as he recalls.

'I heard about this right from an early stage, but most of the girls wouldn't even consider using a man take the photographs, so they looked into every possible way of having a lady photographer taking them. It became evident that my wife Lynda was the only practical option, if she had some guidance along the way on setting up the shoot, because I had been involved with the whole project from the outset. Right away I was contributing my ideas about what could be done. I think they appreciated that, and I had very heavy involvement in the ideas, the situations and the locations.'

But, as Lynda says, they soon found out that it was well-nigh impossible to run a photo-shoot

In the film, Annie and Chris interview several photographers before settling for Lawrence.

without the photographer actually in the room, directing the shots and taking control of the composition.

'We started with Terry outside the room, but it didn't work because he was shouting from behind the door to me, "Just tell her to lift her head, and move it to the left". He was looking through a crack in the door, which seemed so stupid. And so the girls just said "Get in here and take the pictures", and he did just that. He knew exactly what he was doing. I hadn't realised that he had had it all in his head. He's a very organised man and he'd thought about it carefully. He didn't just come in and say, "Oh, I think I'll just take this photograph".'

He was shouting from behind the door to me, "Just tell her to lift her head, and move it to the left" ... [it] seemed so stupid.'

Lynda Logan

The connection between the photographer and the Calendar Girls is in reality much closer than that portrayed in the film. Terry Logan *(below)* is married to Lynda (Miss July). Their daughter, Georgina, is married to Matthew Baker, Angela *(above)* and John's son.

That is a point which Christine Clancy picked upon too, noting the care and thought that Terry had put into the project before anyone had even arrived at his house, Park Grange. 'He's very particular and very precise,' she says. 'We didn't realise before the shoot how much work he had done in the background. He had sorted out all the pictures for everybody before we started. He had produced all these pencil drawings of what he wanted and what it would end up looking like, and in the end he achieved it. So it didn't just happen off the cuff. He knew exactly what he was going to do.'

Certainly Terry had the qualifications and the experience. Before he returned to his native Yorkshire to become a painter, he had worked in

Vancouver as an art director for what was then the world's largest advertising agency, J Walter Thompson. This gave him plenty of experience of working with and photographing women wearing relatively little. He even knew what it was like to work with amateur models against a tight deadline. Once, he had been sent on assignment to photograph a swimwear catalogue on location in Hawaii, only to have the swimwear impounded for a week on arrival by suspicious US customs and to find that, at the time, there were no professional models on the island. 'We had to recruit our own, while the client was going mad asking what we were up to,' he remembers.

Accordingly, he was able to bring this knowledge to bear on the task of producing a witty, dignified and wonderfully composed series of images.

'We started out initially with this room,' he explained, gesturing to the living room, 'the kitchen, studio and the potting shed. We started making a list of scenes for each month. They recruited eleven ladies to portray January to November, because the December one was always going to be the group carol singing. This was going to be outside in the snow with lanterns, but we thought "No, that isn't really realistically ever going to work as a nude picture", so it would have to be carol singing indoors.

'So we had to find eleven different set-ups and eleven different types of craft or pastime that were undertaken by the WI. We had a big brainstorming session to discuss all the options. As each of the possibilities was being suggested, I was weighing up in my mind which physically could be done

Lawrence (Philip Glenister) tentatively introduces his idea.

How the film portrayed setting up the first shot.

Lynda (*below*) was one of the people considered to take the pictures, but it was her husband, Terry, who eventually did the honours.

'[December] was going to be carol singing outside in the snow with lanterns, but we thought "No, that isn't realistically ever going to work as a nude picture".' *Terry Logan*

and which would lend itself to a photograph, and obviously quite a lot of them didn't.'

The Logans' own seventeenth-century farmhouse provided a superb setting, complete with huge oak beams, a massive stone fireplace and stone-flagged country kitchen. Its other great advantage was that its rooms were easily spacious enough for the subjects, and the photographer and his assistant, to move around comfortably. The mullion-windowed farmhouse seemed to have come their way for this very purpose, Lynda believes, as they were actually trying to move out of the area to get nearer to their gallery at Ripley.

'About four different times we were on the verge of buying a house and then something would crop up, and the buyer would drop out for one reason or another. So we moved in here and rented it for a couple of months. Then the owner said he wanted to sell Park Grange while we were in it, and we looked at each other and we made an offer to him. So the house really came to us, we didn't look for it. Then when it came to shooting the calendar, all the photographs were taken in this house. If we'd had a smaller house, we wouldn't have been able to do it.

'We'd only been here five months when John died, though he did see it. He had a pheasant dinner here, which he certainly enjoyed. We didn't understand at the time why the house came to us, but it's certainly repaid us since.'

The apple-press operated by Miss October in the original calendar is a keepsake of the time that the Logans spent in Canada. Terry had made it himself and used it in cider and wine making while they were out there and, when it came time to return he could not bear to throw it out, partly because it taken so much effort to make. So it was transported back over 6,000 miles to Yorkshire and for twenty-five years it was a redundant piece of machinery, pushed from one house to another. The calendar not only revealed its purpose but made the apple-press into a film star, co-starring opposite Helen Mirren in one striking scene. The film company wanted the scene to be authentic and so insured it for £1,000 before shipping it down to Shepperton for the shoot, then returning it.

The equipment used for the shoot was minimal, a twenty-year-old 35mm Nikon and a 1,000-watt tungsten light unit that had nearly been thrown away. 'The cine light was my dad's,' says Matthew. 'He used it when he was taking the Super Eight films of us when we were growing up and on holidays. My mum found it in the loft when she was having a clear-out and gave it to Terry.'

The search for props was relatively straightforward too, as most homes had some of the equipment for jam-making, cake-making, buns and tea. And one prop, the very hefty apple-press that features in both the calendar and the film, eventually justified its 6,000 mile trip to Yorkshire. Terry had made the press himself while living in Vancouver and used it to make wine from windfall apples and grapes. Even when the family decided to return he could not bear to throw it away, and so had been transporting it from one home to another over the past couple of decades, even though it had little purpose in life except taking up a corner of the potting shed.

The other props, which gave the photographs such a distinct image, were the pearls. These were suggested because they are so associated with the 'twinset and sensible shoes' image of the WI that the nakedness of the models so undermined. But the most important symbolically was the sunflower motif that ran throughout the calendar, an emblem of hope and new life.

Emotions amongst the models were mixed, ranging from the relatively relaxed to the frankly frightened. Beryl Bamforth, Miss January, featured in a group shot as the head of a WI meeting, facing towards the naked audience. She says: 'I'm not going to say that I whipped my clothes off and thought nothing of it, but I wasn't wanting to run round hiding myself because there wasn't much

The sunflower in most of the original pictures was actually plastic, with the yellow added to the sepia pictures during the production process.

Chris consults with Lawrence about her shot.

'There was that awful moment when they asked "Who's going next and I said "Me", got my dressing gown off and sat at the piano.' *Angela Baker*

point really. It's not a question of the photographs themselves, but you've got to get it right and poses need re-doing, so you're very exposed to each other as well as the photographer.'

But others were not quite so nonchalant about disrobing. Chris Clancy remembers: 'I don't mind admitting I was terrified. I thought to myself "you must be mad" and I didn't tell a soul until after it was done.' As her husband John drove her up to the photo-session from their home in Skipton, she found herself continually wringing her hands with sheer worry, until he had to tell her to calm down, she was not about to be shot, except with a camera.

Ros Fawcett too had her qualms. 'I was so nervous I kept my trousers on. I thought I was going to strangle myself with them. I was there pretending to be knitting with this blanket up to my chin and down to my ankles, but they made me take my trousers off and pull the blanket down to show my shoulders. But I was glad when it was done.'

Such nervousness did not go unnoticed and everyone did their best to allay the feeling. 'I went second because one girl was really anxious,' says Angela. 'There was that awful moment when they asked "Who's going next?" and I said "Me", got my dressing gown off and sat at the piano.'

Her preparation, she says, was minimal: nothing more than taking her bra off earlier in the day, as advised by Tricia, so that there would be no marks on her skin later in the evening.

'I had no make-up on and I'd got no pearls, and the girls just made me up and did my hair. When I got there I realised how hard Terry and Lynda had been thinking about the shots, the poses and the props. It looked so good. I just thought to myself

that night: "This could really work". And then I just thought: "These girls are all here for me".'

After this example, and a glass or perhaps two of wine to steady the nerves, the shoot proceeded smoothly, just as Terry had planned. 'Once we had got the first couple of shots over with, it just went really well. They were apprehensive more than anything else. They weren't that nervous and I think I made them relax,' he remembers. 'I just kept the whole thing on a professional basis without making cynical or sleazy remarks. This made them relax and we got on with the job.'

Tricia found herself posing with the cider-press, together with some windfall apples and empty wine bottles. The cider-press is a large, hefty item, leading Tricia to quip: 'The bigger the girl, the bigger the prop.' She admits to having felt nervous, momentarily, but felt she could not make a fuss. 'After all, this is what I'd wanted for ages.' So she just put on more lipstick and, without even combing her hair, tried to look unwrinkled.

For Terry, speed was to be the essence of success, arranging his sets and his lighting with a minimum of fuss so that his models never lost confidence. 'I had to direct them very heavily, very strongly and very speedily. There was a very good reason for that: I knew that if they thought about this for too long, they might run out of bottle.

'If I had got all these women here in one night and only got two sets done, and the others had been waiting around all night, I have a feeling that they would have begun to lose their nerve and start getting very apprehensive about it, and maybe even changed their minds. So I planned every shot in my mind beforehand. I knew where I was going to do it, I knew which props I needed and I had them all ready. My wife and I got everything

'The bigger the girl, the bigger the prop.'

Tricia Stewart

'They put their dressing gowns back on, and the next lady came out and we got her ready. The shots were taken at a remarkable speed.' *Terry Logan*

organised, and so I thought "We need to move this smoothly and seamlessly from one set-up into the next one". They put their dressing gowns back on, and the next lady came out and we got her ready. The shots were taken at a remarkable speed.'

In doing this Terry had an accomplice, a tall (nearly six foot) woman friend who could hold the powerful 1,000-watt halogen light. This meant that she could simply move the light in different positions according to his directions, rather than him having to constantly adjust a light-stand. And this was extremely necessary, because the light was so harsh that if it had been applied directly to the models it would have shown up every last wrinkle and blemish.

'To get the correct lighting effect, we had to bounce a light from the ceiling. For every shot my lighting lady moved it to my instruction to a slightly different position, and she kept moving around the subject as I kept taking photographs,' say Terry. 'For each particular set-up we did, we had twenty or thirty lighting variations of it, which was absolutely invaluable and it didn't take that long to do. If we had done it the traditional way in a studio, it would have taken probably half a day to do each one. This way we ran through them really quickly, giving them no chance to back out.'

Even so, some of his sitters still found the experience rather strange. Christine recalls: 'In my first set of photographs, I was playing darts, because

the WI do actually play darts in a league. It was very funny. It's a bizarre thing to do when you think about it, isn't it? Standing there facing a dartboard which was hanging on a friend's door, with her husband standing at the back of you with a camera. It's not normal really, is it? But we were never there on our own, you know, everybody was there together laughing at you and poking fun, making silly jokes all the time.'

And it is the giddy excitement that they had that autumn evening that sticks in Ros's mind too, despite her nerves. 'It was a lot of fun. We'd be giggling in our dressing gowns when we took the shots in the potting shed and laughing about what the village would think if they knew what we got up to on a Sunday night,' she says.

That first October evening proved very successful, yielding seven different set-ups in little over three hours, with only slight corrections needed to around three of them, while a couple needed redoing entirely. One of these unfortunately featured Christine playing darts, and this was one that Terry had doubts about even when it was first suggested.

'I was rather over-exposed, you might say,' says Christine. 'I wasn't throwing the darts at the camera, I was stood with my back to the camera taking them out of the dartboard, looking over my shoulder, and I didn't like that very much.'

A swift discussion among the friends reached the conclusion that the images did not fit with what the calendar was meant to portray, and instead Christine ended up with a teapot. This, she says, had the advantage of being rather warmer, since it was photographed in the kitchen and in front of the Aga, even though the set-up had its own problems:

'It was quite difficult to do, really. It was a big old teapot that we borrowed from the village hall.

'It's a bizarre thing to do when you think about it, isn't it? Standing there facing a dartboard which was hanging on a friend's door, with her husband standing at the back of you with a camera. It's not normal really, is it?' *Chris Clancy*

I was pouring into little cups and it just kept running over. So we had to tip it back into the teapot and pour it again, because Terry actually wanted tea to be pouring out,' Christine says. At one point Lynda nipped out to the shop for iced fairy cakes, titivating them with cherries from her Christmas cake supplies for extra effect.

After three shoots in all, the final poses had been decided, and the team then had to choose

which shots to use. In each case, Terry selected three or four of the best from which the girls could choose the image to be used, and then there was a committee at Terry and Lynda's to work out the next stage. Again, the village was able to provide a couple of journalists to advise and also a former advertising executive, Nick McGooligan, who had set up a holiday company in the nearby village of Embsay. Not only were they convinced that the calendar could work, but McGooligan was prepared to back it all the way. He not only paid the reprographic fees and the printer's bill, but he also made his warehouse available so that the calendars could be stored there rather than in garages and garden sheds. But the advisers also pointed out that it was far too late to get the calendar out in time to sell in 1999, because there were only two months left in which to design and print it. Instead, they advised that the calendar should be targeted at 2000, the Millennium year, and that the secret should be kept for a few months yet.

Another meeting was also needed to decide what captions should go with the images. Some ideas were still around from the first meeting at the Devonshire, but they were able to persuade a journalist from the yoga class to offer his thoughts, and there were also recipe books and WI publications from which to crib quotes. These caused a lot

Tricia had wanted her image with the cider-press to be the opening lines of Keats's *Ode to Autumn*: 'Season of mist and mellow fruitfulness'. Instead she got 'Fruity and full-bodied'.

of hilarity, as many were ancient issues of Home & Country, the WI magazine, dating from the sixties. These were filled with women in frocks and high-heeled shoes, busy cooking, baking, jam-making and hoovering away to make the perfect oasis of calm for the man when he returned from the office. Since all the women involved had jobs and businesses of their own, there was little of this in evidence at the Rylstone & District branch some thirty years later.

Tricia had wanted her image with the cider-press to be captioned with the opening lines of Keats's *Ode to Autumn*: 'Season of mist and mellow fruitfulness'. Instead she got 'Fruity and full-bodied'. Christine's tea-pouring with the cherried buns was captioned 'One lump or two?', while Angela's piano-playing was underscored with a line from Jerusalem: 'And did the countenance divine shine forth'. The captions often pointed up the visual puns. Lynda, photographed in a characteristic pose while painting at the easel, was 'A nude painting'. By the time the committee got to December, the Christmas shot of the nine women draped around the inglenook obscured by

Terry and Lynda Logan have kept a fascinating array of items from the calendar's history, including (*right*) the scribbled ideas from the night of caption-writing.

song sheets and tinsel, the caption seemed obvious: 'Happy Nude Year'.

By now Terry had enough material to show his models just what they had got themselves into. He did a mock-up of what the calendar should look like when it was produced. The reaction was one of pleasant shock.

'When you saw the mock-up, it really made you think "My God, this is happening!". They looked wonderful. He'd done a superb job, he really had,' Christine remembers.

'When you saw the mock-up, it really made you think "My God, this is happening!". They looked wonderful.' *Christine Clancy*

Ros was impressed too, 'I thought it was just lovely. I thought that, for middle-aged women, he'd really made us look good. We didn't look tarty or anything. We looked classy, and there was a lot of humour with the captions underneath.'

Lynda's reaction was the more emotional: 'When I saw it, I cried. I just said "That's absolutely fantastic". He'd worked so hard at it.'

Other reactions were rather more prosaic. Terry Fletcher, who had first heard of the idea at the yoga class, was overwhelmed with surprise. 'I was asked to go to Terry's house and, with very sheepish expressions on their faces, they slid this calendar across the table at me. I nearly fell off my chair in astonishment. I never thought they'd do it, and here it was: the finished article sitting there large as life.'

Further improvements were to come, thanks to modern printing technology. Terry explains: 'We got the repro house to digitally lift out the sunflowers in colour because Georgina thought that it would look really good against the sepia. And it really does. It gives a great lift. The sepia idea came from the photo processor.'

While Terry organised the printing of the calendar, he came across a problem that dismayed many of the girls. Angela says: 'We were going to have a thousand printed because we thought we might be able to sell that many if we were lucky. But the printer said he couldn't run the press for just a thousand, we'd have to go to three thousand.'

Journalist Terry Fletcher, who was by now acting as unofficial public relations consultant, also remembers what a bombshell this proved to be. 'We were sitting round Terry's table that night when they showed me the calendar. They had originally thought they might sell one or two hundred copies to a few friends and neighbours. But then the minimum print run was three thousand, and they were just dumbfounded. They couldn't see how they could get rid of them, because their original idea was just to take them round local shops in the boot of their car and try and persuade someone to take half a dozen. Now they just had

Angela, Lynda and Tricia's daughter Lizzie at the Logans' kitchen table.

Annie goes in search of sponsorship.

visions of having their garages and lofts stuffed with these calendars for years.'

The calendar also needed sponsorship to pay for the costs of production, though many of the girls were able to contribute, either personally or through their own businesses. The original calendar shows just how modest and local the enterprise was. Ros Fawcett's business, the Vogue Fashion Agency, is up there together with Tricia's medical software company, but the only national business from the thirty-odd sponsors was a quarry company, Tilcon.

The big boost came through the local pub, which involved its brewery, Jennings. Tricia had contacted a director and, through this, the calendar idea had landed on the desk of Graham Kennedy, then working in marketing.

'At first we weren't sure if it was genuine or someone was winding us up,' he says. 'But I arranged to meet Tricia at the Devonshire Arms, and she furtively brought a brown envelope out from under the table and showed us some of the early shots. I thought it was a fantastic idea, a fabulous way of supporting the cause. It was unique because of the fusty image of the WI and the reason for doing it was rooted in personal tragedy. They had lost someone in that region who was very highly regarded.

'What struck me was that there would be massive interest from the media and from the public,

'I arranged to meet Tricia at the Devonshire Arms, and she furtively brought a brown envelope out from under the table and showed us some of the early shots.'

Graham Kennedy

Angela with some of the staff at Jennings Brewery.

and it was something they were underestimating. They thought they might be able to sell a couple of thousand calendars and raise a few thousand pounds, but I thought they could raise a great deal of money if they approached things in a structured way. They wanted advice on how to publicise the calendar and were thinking about a few lines in the local newspaper, but I said they should be looking at a media launch and alerting the national media.'

Jennings also offered to handle the mail-order side, which came as a relief to many. 'We thought that we would end up walking into post offices and newsagents all over Yorkshire with these calendars under our arms, asking them to sell them for us on "sale or return",' Ros says.

The calendar also needed the goodwill of the Women's Institute, if it was to bill itself as the 'Alternative WI Calendar', and the Leukaemia Research Fund (LRF). Both were to prove supportive when they saw the calendar. An early, nervous

> 'There we were, these middle-aged women showing this guy in his early thirties our nude calendar.'
>
> Angela Baker

meeting at the Ripon headquarters of the regional federation of the WI raised no objections (one lady said she wanted to give a copy to her husband for Christmas), but a trip to London won the backing of both bodies.

At LRF they met the press officer, Andrew Trehearne, who promised to help and to liaise with Jennings to maximise the publicity. Angela says: 'There we were, these middle-aged women showing this guy in his early thirties our nude calendar. I always remember that he came down in the lift with us to escort us off the premises. I think he was scared, poor fella. He said he wasn't, but he

The Devonshire Arms, where so many events in the calendar's history took place.

did think "Heavens, they don't know what they've done, they have no idea what this is going to be like". And it's a good job we didn't.'

The launch date was chosen to coincide with the LRF's annual conference in nearby Leeds, which would be a week later. The original idea, according to Terry Fletcher, had been to hold a news conference on Sunday so it would be what is termed a 'Sunday-for-Monday' story and get the best coverage in newspapers that are customarily desperate for news. But the Devonshire Arms could not cope with a Sunday launch and so it was launched on a Monday, but not before two national papers had approached them. The *Guardian* and the *Daily Mail* both wanted to break the embargo (the official publication date) and print a story on the Monday of the launch.

Terry Fletcher says: 'Trish rang me and asked whether she should let the newspapers have it and,

'I thought that would it would be a one-day wonder. It would be in those two papers and no-one would turn up at the press conference.'
Terry Fletcher

while any journalist gets upset about embargo breaking, I actually advised them to break their own.' Terry argued that getting spreads in two such widely read papers was a rather good start, adding, 'If the Queen Mum dies tomorrow, you won't get anything'.

He adds: 'I thought that it would be a one-day wonder. It would be in those two papers and no-one would turn up at the press conference.' He was wrong. Very wrong.

media frenzy

When the ladies of Rylstone & District WI drop everything for their traditional crafts, 'Jam and Jerusalem' will never be the same again.

Frontispiece, The Alternative WI Calendar

The launch of the calendar was frenetic, an omen of what was to come. Tricia got the first hint: by nine o'clock she had already done six radio interviews, and the press launch was not until eleven.

Although the story was already in two national papers, the demand for any snippet of news, any soundbite from the models themselves, was feverish. The press releases and a photograph from the calendar had been sent out to all the national newspapers and the broadcast media. So, while the press might have to wait for the conference at the Devonshire Arms, the radio broadcasters had no such qualms, and the only phone number they had was Tricia's.

She was up in time to admire the write-ups in the *Daily Mail* and *Guardian*, with headlines such as 'From pinnies to pin-ups', but found it nearly impossible to get dressed as the phone rang incessantly. Meanwhile, the Devonshire Arms was being decked out with sunflowers, various snacks and enlargements of the calendar images.

Angela says: 'We had this idea that there probably wouldn't be very many people there, and we'd be drinking the wine and eating the nibbles ourselves.'

The idea was that Tricia would make the opening speech and then the rest of the team would march out, dressed in black but with a small sunflower on

Beryl and Lynda, astonished at the newspaper coverage.

the lapel, to the strains of Neil Sedaka's *Calendar Girl* to face questions. In fact, they faced a mob.

'It was mayhem really. There were satellite dishes, journalists, photographers. There were people shouting "Will you do this?" and "Can you speak to us?". We were on *Look North* (the local television news) at lunchtime and we were on the Six o'Clock BBC national news,' says Angela.

Terry Logan has mixed feelings about the launch, believing that a certain degree of naivety meant they came close to losing what turned out to be a great source of money for charity: reproduction fees for the photographs themselves. There was also the problem of not having enough copies of the calendar to hand out to everybody.

'The printer was still putting them together, and he managed to rush 100 copies to us on the day of the launch, which the press eagerly devoured. There were promotional photos all over the media, which was the big mistake that we made. We should have controlled those photographs,

'They would insist on taking our photographs at the bus stop … all these photographers standing in the middle of the road had to leap out of the way every time a lorry came past. It seemed crazy really.'

Beryl Bamforth

and after about twenty-four hours we did. We appointed a press photo agency to handle them for us. But unfortunately the first 100 calendars had already disappeared, and the photos were used willy-nilly for quite a few months without any payment. We had to do a lot of serious talking to some photo agencies to get them to start paying for the use of the photographs, because all the money should have been going to the Leukaemia Research Fund and they were getting away without paying.'

Beryl Bamforth's memory of the event was that everything seemed rather off-kilter, as if it was happening to someone else. 'It all seemed quite unreal. People were saying: "You go and be interviewed on the telephone or on the radio, or talk to this television station or that newspaper". They would insist on taking our photographs at the bus stop in Cracoe. They obviously thought it was a very quiet road. But there were lorries coming down from the quarry, and all these photographers standing in the middle of the road had to leap out of the way every time one came past. It seemed crazy really.'

The immediate, intense media coverage in the film was no exaggeration.

Nor did it stop that morning. In the afternoon, various members of the group found themselves

being ferried to television studios in Leeds to be interviewed live. It was, recalls Ros, a great relief to return home, and to do the Monday night pub quiz as usual. Even then the pressure just did not ease off: Tricia found herself doing a live interview with Radio Chicago just outside the bar on her husband's mobile phone while Angela answered her questions in the quiz. Tricia was already developing an ability to conduct interviews in unusual situations that would serve her well.

The next day started bright and early with a slot on *GMTV*, the early-morning news magazine programme, with interviews in Terry and Lynda's lounge, the scene for many of the calendar shots. Only then could the girls examine their news coverage. They were in every paper.

As Graham Kennedy noted: 'It was such a strong story that even newspapers that felt aggrieved about the embargo being broken still had no option but to run it.'

> Tricia found herself doing a live interview with Radio Chicago just outside the bar on her husband's mobile phone while Angela answered her questions in the quiz.

And that kept up the momentum, so that even more radio stations were pressing for interviews, people were ordering calendars and more television shows were demanding appearances. And, in between answering two telephones, Tricia managed a telephone interview on national radio with the veteran host Jimmy Young who, professional as ever, went right to the kernel of the calendar. He recognised that its prime aim was to raise money for research into leukaemia. This was an important consideration in deciding whether to accept invitations or not, because it was plain that many

One of the digressions from real life for the sake of dramatic tension was to pitch Chris and Annie against the WI.

journalists would simply want the girls to defend nudity, whereas the point of publicity was to sell calendars. And that is just what it did. Within the first seven days, the calendar sold its first print run of 3,000 and generated orders for another 3,000.

But what happened then defied the normal logic of the media, says Terry Fletcher. 'All the reporters were saying: "What is there to do? This story has been done." And there really was no follow-up. This was partly because we prevented this by getting the local vicar on our side, so he wasn't going to say anything against the calendar.

'We also got the WI on our side, because the fear you have is that you've got a positive story one day, and then for the follow-up somebody will go looking for the knocking copy. And it didn't happen. So the story that appeared the next day was exactly the same as the one that appeared the first day, and the following day it was still more or less

the same. It defied the law of gravity as a story because it never moved on. There was nothing new to say, but it just kept appearing every day. I can only assume that we had an incredibly flat news week,' Terry Fletcher concludes.

'We got the local vicar on our side, so he wasn't going to say anything against the calendar.'

Terry Fletcher

Flat news week or not, the calendar was well set up for the Leukaemia Research Fund conference in Leeds that next weekend. The launch was further helped by a flood of coverage in the weekend papers and helpful mentions on national radio by Terry Wogan, who kept stimulating even more phone calls and letters by telling listeners that the calendar had sold out.

By the following week the girls were beginning to get some sense of the odd places the calendar would take them. A young female researcher from a Thames Television programme, *Living Room*, rang wanting some ladies from the calendar to come down to its studio and make a typical WI pudding. 'Bread and butter pudding?'. 'No'. 'Jam roly-poly?' 'No.' 'Spotted dick?' (Choked giggling.) 'Yes.' So it was that Angela, Tricia and Lynda found themselves on an early midweek train from Skipton to London, the first of many. None of them had actually made spotted dick, but were willing to play along with the humour for the sake of a free plug, and so they took a plastic bag containing a pudding that Angela's mum had made. And, to make best use of the free train tickets, they put in some calendars to deliver to the Queen and Queen Mother (both members of the Sandringham WI) at Buckingham Palace.

Despite a bomb scare at King's Cross, the girls landed spic and span at the television studios, where the researcher welcomed them, checked out the spotted dick (more giggling fits) and sent them off to the make-up department before their appearance. As they were waiting in the Green Room, the call came through from the Queen's press secretary to confirm that they could deliver the calendars to the palace.

Then it was showtime. While Angela managed to make the serious points about the calendar and its purpose, Lynda fulfilled the producer's hopes with a series of double-entendres about spotted dick and how you needed two hands to handle it; that is, to tie on the greaseproof paper. In fact, she got rather carried away, according to Angela.

'It was just a studio set. The taps were there but no sink, and we had to look busy, so we were just cleaning away when Lynda said, "Close that window,

Lynda fulfilled the producer's hopes with a series of double-entendres about spotted dick ... in fact, she got rather carried away.

there's a real draught". After we made the spotted dick, we put it on a dish and cut it into slices, and as soon as we were off air the whole crew descended and ate everything, even though it was stone cold. There wasn't even a currant left.'

After feeding the plainly under-fed television technicians, the trio went to Buckingham Palace, where the equerry quipped, 'Excuse the pun, but her Majesty does like to keep abreast of events.' Not only did they deliver calendars but they also managed to sell copies to the Queen's private detective and two policemen at the palace gate. After a swift cup of tea in a café, they were off in a taxi to the next gig, an appearance on *Backstage* at BBC Digital, rather a comedown after Thames Television.

Are Leo Sayer's luscious curls real or woven ? Lynda Logan knows. Left to right, Tricia, Angela, Leo, Lynda.

Isn't he dreamy? Terry Wogan would be a constant help with his numerous mentions of the calendar and the cause.

'We asked for a dressing room and all there was was a toilet,' says Tricia. 'But we weren't too worried because the taxi driver had told us no-one watched the channel anyway.'

But still, it was another chance to push the calendar and it included an opportunity to sing with Leo Sayer and for Lynda to ask him whether his full head of tight curly hair was real.

'We came back absolutely exhausted but it was truly brilliant,' was Tricia's verdict. Just as well. In the year to come they would be going down to London at least once a week and it would all become a familiar routine. 'We got to know the woman who made bacon sandwiches at Skipton Station, and befriended the guard on the first train out down to London. He'd get the train to go faster so we could make the connections,' says Angela.

This was only part of a life that was becoming increasingly crowded and hectic, with appearances at shows to sell and promote the calendars, and managing what was becoming a storming success.

As Graham Kennedy drily observes: 'It exceeded our expectations. The switchboard at Jennings was blocked and we had to put in an extra couple of dedicated phone lines. Staff who were working part time in the visitors' centre ended up working full time and into the night taking orders and sending them out.'

Jennings would keep sending for new supplies in whatever vehicle was available, a delivery van if possible but sometimes just an estate car which would make its way back to the brewery's offices in Cockermouth with its suspension complaining under the weight as it travelled to the far side of the Lake District.

But Jennings was not dealing with all the calendars, because thousands of requests and letters came through the post, with addresses such as

Keeping up with demand – just. Tricia, Angela and Lynda load up with a new batch of calendars from the warehouse.

'Miss October, Yorkshire' and 'WI Calendar, England'.

'We were like a fire-chain, getting them out of the warehouse and into people's cars. We needed about six trips at a time because there were only so many calendars you could get in without damaging the suspension, then we'd take them out and pack them at Angela's,' says Tricia.

'We used to sit at the kitchen table signing and sending calendars. They weren't vacuum sealed at first, so we had to use freezer bags and put on a Leukaemia Research Fund sticker. We had to order 3,000 calendars at first, and then 5,000 because we thought there was a demand. Then we went to 10,000, and we were petrified. When we got to order 20,000, the printers sealed them and put little pictures on the back.'

But Angela points out that it was not just the labour of getting the calendars out that was exhausting: there was an emotional element to it too.

'Some letters were from older ladies in the WI

Thousands of requests and letters came through the post, with addresses such as 'Miss October, Yorkshire' and 'WI Calendar, England'.

saying "Good on you, this is just what the WI needed. What a shame I never thought about doing it". Others were from people who had been bereaved through cancer, saying "What a memorial for John Baker. He must have been a great guy for you to do all this". Sometimes they were really funny and sometimes we cried, so we used to have a packet of tissues on the table.'

A common reaction was for middle-aged women to write in to say how the confidence of the women in the calendar had restored their own flagging self-esteem. One woman from Bristol in her mid-forties wrote: 'How absolutely bloody marvellous! I have no intention of reaching my fifties, sixties, seventies or more and lying down for the rest of my life, and I know that a lot of other women out there need to see that they aren't expected to either.' Another letter, from Liverpool, said: 'It makes us oldies feel better about ourselves, quite uplifted in fact.'

Some even found the calendar therapeutic. A man in the Orkney Islands wrote to say that it had helped to convince his forty-seven-year-old wife that she was no less desirable for having recently had a mastectomy. Another man saw the calendar as a blow against the prevailing conventions of beauty, writing: 'How wonderful to see real women instead of stick insects with pouty lips and pipe-cleaner legs.'

There were plenty of lighter moments too, such as the Erotic Oscar. Tricia explains: 'Calls came to

anyone they could find. If they couldn't find us, they'd ring the pub. One time, the girl behind the bar took a call and said she thought we'd been awarded a Rustic Oscar, and I thought: "That's fantastic, us being country people". But when I rang back there was music in the background and it said "Welcome to the world of erotica". It turned out it we'd been awarded the Erotic Oscar by *Loaded* magazine, and they invited us to the Sex Maniacs Ball to accept it. But we thought that would not go with our WI image.'

Ros had ensured that the calendar got a good airing by sending it to anyone she thought might promote it, with Radio Two presenters such as Ken Bruce, Sarah Kennedy and Michael Parkinson featuring strongly. Terry Wogan, for instance, kept plugging it. Comedienne Jo Brand got a copy too, and incorporated it into her stand-up show with the joke that she was going to appear as Miss December, photographed behind a bungalow. Favourite writers such as Victoria Wood and Alan Bennett, and actresses such as Maureen Lipman and Glenda Jackson (a government minister by this time) also got a copy.

Alan Bennett wrote to warn them against being 'seduced by celebrity', and that Victoria sponges and pickles were far more worthwhile, but Ros feels there was little likelihood of that. 'We were

Fellow Yorkshireman Michael Parkinson provided more publicity through the airwaves.

asked to speak to the Monday Club locally, and to a group called the Men's Forum with just twenty there. But then you would go somewhere else and find yourself talking to thousands.'

Alongside these appearances, the pressure from the media intensified. The BBC now wanted to make a documentary about the phenomenon, and Channel Four were keen to make a film about the Dales that would be presented by Richard Whiteley. In the course of discussions with Whiteley, the girls talked about Terry Wogan and how he had helped through his constant mentions. The result was an invitation to be on Whiteley's quiz show *Countdown* when it was filmed at the Leeds television studios and when the much-admired Wogan would be a guest. So off they trooped in their by-now-customary uniform of black dresses plus sunflower, together with Terry Logan, determined to get a shot of 'Wogan meets Logan'. The idea was to take Wogan by surprise, which they did,

'It turned out it we'd been awarded the Erotic Oscar by *Loaded* magazine. They invited us to the Sex Maniacs Ball to accept it. But we thought that would not go with our WI image.' *Tricia Stewart*

The Cracoe postman, Roy Harrison, is one of only two people in the movie to appear as himself (the other is the TV show host Jay Leno). Now, he says, he finds that cars going through the village sound their horns in recognition, 'and I've no idea who they are.'

Roy's fame is a measure of the Calendar Girls' gratitude because his workload suddenly multiplied overnight as the calendar took off and he never complained. But he has served the little community of Cracoe for more than twenty-three years and was not going to let something like the calendar put him off his stride. 'It was just like Christmas,' he says. 'Only a bit earlier. And longer.' So he kept delivering the bundles of letters and calendar requests by the hundred.

'Some letters were just addressed to "Miss May" or "Miss October", or just "Calendar, Yorkshire",' he recalls. And, as he knew all the Calendar Girls by name and sight, he was one of the few able to deliver the letters personally.

The Calendar Girls say they always knew when they had a particularly prestigious invitation because Roy would deliver it with the words 'You've all got one'.

Roy was one of the many people thanked with a party held at a marquee in Burnsall. He remembers the evening as a marvellous climax to the whole experience, and found himself autographing calendars for Celia Imrie and Penelope Wilton.

emerging one by one, after an introduction by Whiteley, to kiss the Irish celebrity.

The girls were keen to exploit their fame to raise more money for the Leukaemia Research Fund with more products. One that bit the dust after an abortive afternoon's recording was a CD in which they would all sing songs such as Sedaka's *Calendar Girl*, but the idea for a Christmas card in much the same vein as the calendar proved a winner. A local businessman offered to sponsor it by printing 50,000 cards for free.

As summer came round, the girls decided to go on the road, visiting the agricultural shows that abound in Yorkshire and are the natural habitat of the WI, which was originally formed with the motto 'For Home and Country' to encourage rural crafts. Ros's husband Chris runs a tent and marquee factory, so he designed and made them a marquee with a large sunflower on it, from which to sell the calendars. It was at the Great Yorkshire Show, when they sold 3,000 calendars over three days, that they met Prince Charles.

Christine Clancy recalls: 'He wanted to meet us, so we were sent to the Prince's Trust Tent. When we arrived there was no sign of anybody, but a steward explained that Prince Charles was running late, so we had to hurry off to find him. There was a great mass of people in front of us, so we thought we wouldn't get anywhere near him, but a policeman walking past asked "Are you them women on the calendar?". "Yes," we explained, "we're supposed to be going to see Prince Charles but we can't get anywhere near." He just turned and shouted "Make way for the Calendar Girls", and the crowd parted.'

At this point Lynda discovered she had a royal admirer. 'He told me that my photograph was his favourite. Someone asked him why: is she your favourite because you'd like to paint her or would you like to have lessons from her? And he said "She'd be far too expensive for me either way".'

But the shows also meant that the Girls met people whose lives had been damaged by leukaemia. At the Great Yorkshire Show, for instance,

Wogan meets Logan.

Angela accepts a cheque at the Kilnsey Agricultural show.

one woman explained how her own case was in remission, while another described how she had just lost her daughter to the disease, leaving her granddaughter without a mother.

In the midst of all this activity, Tricia took a call from a film producer, Suzanne Mackie of Harbour Pictures. Mackie had finally received the calendar that she had ordered way back in April when screenwriter Juliette Towhidi had pointed out the very first national news report.

She explains: 'I didn't really know what the story could be, but then Tricia sent me the actual calendar through the post. I thought, "This really pushes all the buttons for me as a woman. It makes me laugh and feel very triumphant for them." But it takes a lot more than humour to create a story that can translate to film. Then I turned the calendar over and realised that the reason they had done it was that one of their husbands had died of cancer. That very small but universal tragedy had precipitated these middle-aged women to do something daring and brave. There was my story on a plate.'

The calendar had Tricia's number on the back, so Suzanne rang her. 'I asked her if anyone had approached her to do a film and she said no. She had been approached to do everything else: magazines, books, charitable openings.'

But Tricia felt that the decision should rest with Angela and her two children, who were still struggling with their loss and unsure whether they wanted a film to be made. As Matthew puts it: 'At first we weren't keen on letting someone film what was our private story. But then we thought we should continue talking.'

So Suzanne and Juliette made the journey up to Cracoe to meet Angela, together with Lynda and Terry. It soon turned out, Suzanne says, that there was a bond between them.

'At the time my mother was going into a hospice, she was fifty-nine. The minute I mentioned that, Angela realised the pain that I was going through and therefore I couldn't possibly tell that side of the story in an insensitive way, and she felt deeply sad for me. And I felt the same for her and how on earth could we not respect each other, and what the other had gone through. I think she felt that I was sent to her.

> 'Angela realised the pain that I was going through and therefore I couldn't possibly tell that side of the story in an insensitive way.'
>
> *Suzanne Mackie*

'I think when you're going through that, there's a really strong sense of people needing to band together, to have an outlet to tell what it's like to lose someone you love. I was going through it at that moment, and everyone will go through it at some time. That's why it's important to get that side of the story told honestly and poignantly.

'Angela showed me the boxes and boxes of letters she'd received, and I thought: "There are people like me all over the world".'

Angela also warmed to the film producers, but was uncertain. 'Because it was so soon after John had died, I couldn't think of anything about him being on the screen, and also Rachel and Matthew said they couldn't either. But they were so nice, and they said there would be proper contracts and they would stick to their side of the bargain. We just built up a relationship and a trust with them. We realised that if it was done properly and it was successful, we could raise a lot of money.'

Lawrence, Chris and Annie at the hospital. Recent events in Suzanne Mackie's own life pursuaded Angela that this part of the story would be handled sensitively.

For the moment it was decided that the whole question of the film should be put on hold while the family and film producers had their discussion. Meanwhile, the team got on with a crowded autumn schedule that included being filmed by the BBC as they took part in a fashion show at the Savoy, attended the Woman of the Year Lunch, appeared at Leeds City Varieties, and presented a large cheque to the Leukaemia Research Fund at the Kilnsey Show.

The Calendar Girls had become much in demand for modelling and the *Woman's Journal* was one of several magazines that decided that mature women could show clothes off more realistically to the buying public. They rehearsed by modelling the day before for Marks & Spencer and the *Yorkshire Post*, which photographed them wearing the latest M&S range. Here Beryl showed

'Angela showed me the boxes and boxes of letters she'd received, and I thought "There are people like me all over the world".'

Suzanne Mackie

that she could fill a pair of black leather trousers with style. Christened Biker Beryl for the day, she remarked that she preferred 'something baggy and terribly comfortable'.

The *Woman's Journal* fashion show was a far bigger affair, made even more tense by having a BBC film crew asking questions on the train down. Ros reckons their role was 'to show what the clothes looked like on ordinary people'. She particularly remembers the final show.

Off to the Savoy. The ladies, now in demand for fashion shows, here model at the *Woman's Journal* show.

'Because I'm the smallest, I had to lead our lot out. Well, I'm not exactly model material, but it was really good fun and everyone cheered and clapped. It was so exhilarating, though we looked a state in what they put us in. They sent out the gorgeous models first, wearing the same clothes that we were in, and we were supposed to show what the ordinary woman would look like. Well, did we!

'We had to walk out with attitude and push our way through past the models to the sound of *Sexy Thing*. We now joke how we're the kiss of death to the fashion industry because *Woman's Journal* has closed since and M&S had a rotten year that year. Some of the girls also modelled for C&A and now that's closed down.'

Two weeks later, and the team were back at the Savoy for the Woman of the Year Lunch, an event at which 500 of Britain's leading women are invit-ed to celebrate each other's achievements and to raise money for charity. Maureen Lipman, the Hull-born actress, had invited them and so they sat at her table. Apparently one of the greatest thrills was to sit next to Linda Gray, who played Sue Ellen in the daddy of all soaps, *Dallas*. Ros, not given to overstatement, described it as 'dreamlike'.

But then, in October, Jennings had to deliver some difficult news: it could no longer handle mail orders for the calendar because it was getting busy with its Christmas trade. There were no com-plaints. The brewery had taken on the job and, in the words of one Calendar Girl, 'kept everyone sane'. It had sent out 56,000 calendars and, because the printing was paid for and because it donated its own workforce free, that meant it raised more than £250,000 for charity.

The girls debated whether or not to employ a firm to deal with orders, but Terry had already

Angela with Maureen Lipman at the Woman of the Year Lunch.

made enquiries and found it would have cost too much. There would not have been any money left for the charity.

By now Angela's work at the tourist information centre had stopped for winter, and she took on the task of organising the response to the orders which just kept coming through.

'We were receiving 300 to 450 letters a day, and we became absolutely dab hands at distribution. We did it every day right up until Christmas Eve, a total of 32,000 for the year,' she says. 'I had to have cortisone injections in one elbow. The doctor said I had "calendar elbow" because I had just been packing calendars and boxes, taking them from the garage to the house and then up to the post office.'

But again community spirit proved invaluable. Tricia remembers: 'We had a guy from round the corner who used to come round every now and again, and sit in the corner all day packing them.'

The others helped too, with Ros taking calendars to her dress agency to fill envelopes during quiet moment, while Christine and John Clancy took home piles of calendars.

There was a further complication, adds Tricia. 'The Post Office wouldn't sort us out a franking system because we'd have had to register as a business, so all the envelopes had to have stamps stuck on them.'

But it is touching what people will do for a good cause, says Angela. 'The post offices were brilliant. Debbie and Chris Davey at the post office in Grassington told us to bring the envelopes sorted by weight and they used to bill us for them. Then at night they used to stick on the stamps on while watching television together. They did that for two months.

'Debbie was expecting a second baby and actually went into labour on the night they were showing our documentary on the BBC. She just said "I can't have this baby yet, I've got to watch

Chris Clancy and the *Dallas* star Linda Gray.

Right Grassington Post Office

'We were all getting pretty exhausted by this stage. It was taking over our lives completely. It was a daily routine of humping great bundles of calendars around.'   *Terry Logan*

this programme". We all thought she should call the baby Stamp because she'd stuck on so many.'

By now, with Christmas approaching, the momentum seemed to be slowing down. Terry wanted to avoid ending up with thousands of unsold calendars, and so put in their last order for 20,000 calendars at the beginning of December.

'We thought that when January arrived that would be it and there would be no more requests, but how wrong can you be? It didn't really matter whether it was January or July, the orders just kept on coming in, and we could have easily sold another 20,000.

But we were all getting pretty exhausted by this stage. It was taking over our lives completely. It was a daily routine of humping great bundles of calendars around. They were very heavy. Angela's house looked like a Royal Mail sorting office, stacked as it was with huge mountains of calendars in envelopes waiting to go to the post. So we stopped. We told everybody just before Christmas that we had sold our last calendars and that was it. It did quieten off, but we were still getting a lot of requests and we couldn't satisfy them.'

In the midst of this appeared Warren Hoge, a reporter for the *New York Times* based in London. For months he had been trying to get up to Yorkshire to cover the story of the calendar, but each time had been diverted onto other stories,

mainly peace talks in Northern Ireland. But finally he and his photographer were able to make the train journey north. Warren made his mark at Skipton Station by wearing a pink shirt and matching socks, not a common sight in North Yorkshire. Although the Women's Institute started in Canada, there is no equivalent in the United States, so the Americans were given a crash course about the WI and village life. They were taken to the monthly WI meeting, shown the Rylstone duck pond, with an evening visit to the Devonshire Arms, which was packed with locals playing darts and dominoes.

Angela and Tricia went down to London later that month to discuss a possible deal with what Angela had thought was Floyd PR. In fact, it was Freud PR, one of the top London agencies with clients including Pepsi, Unilever, Channel 4, Geri Halliwell and Chris Evans. Over breakfast in Sloane Square, the agency team explained that they wanted the Calendar Girls to promote a household product (no names, no pack drill) in a billboard advertisement that would be a spoof of a recent anti-fur poster. Commissioned by People for the Ethical Treatment of Animals, this showed naked supermodels such as Naomi Campbell with the line 'We'd rather go naked than wear fur'.

Handing over the cheque to Leukaemia Research Fund.

Angela at the opening of the haemotology outpatient department at Leeds General Infirmary.

But back in Cracoe, it seemed that, once the BBC documentary had been shown, the main event to look forward to was officially handing over a big cheque to the Leukaemia Research Fund. As ever, Jennings and Graham Kennedy did the honours, decking out the Devonshire Arms at Cracoe for the occasion and sending out the press releases. The January event was not just about handing over the money. It was an opportunity to thank so many of the people that had made it possible to raise the massive sum of £331,200.

Douglas Osborne, the chief executive of the Fund, accepted the cheque on behalf of the charity. 'I have been in the charity sphere for some time but I have never come across anything quite like this,' he says. 'Imitation is said to be the sincerest form of flattery but, although there have been many attempts to copy the idea, none has had the

'I have been in the charity sphere for some time but I have never come across anything quite like this. Imitation is said to be the sincerest form of flattery but, although there have been many attempts to copy the idea, none has had the same impact.'   *Douglas Osborne*

same impact. The publicity is probably worth as much again to the charity because we don't spend a lot of money on advertising. It's doubly valuable because we do need to be known, and the coverage throughout the media, from local newspapers to national television, has a lasting effect that is vital to us.'

Meanwhile, Eileen Meadmore, the past chairman of the National Federation of the WI, simply said: 'Thank you very much for the change of image.'

Angela teased the local press, saying that though the calendars were all sold, the girls were looking at other projects. 'Watch this space,' she told them, thinking only of the billboard posters. In fact, she spoke more truly than she could know.

At that stage, the calendar had sold 88,000 copies. Pirelli sold 44,000.

"All the News That's Fit to Print"

The New York Times

Late National Edition

Washington and Oregon: Cloudy with drizzle in the west. Intervals of sun, continued cool in the eastern sections. Little change tomorrow. Weather map and details are on Page 22.

VOL. CXLIX .... No. 51,276 | SUNDAY, JANUARY 23, 2000 | Printed in Tacoma | FOUR DOLLARS

Prosecutors Portray the Strands Of a Bin Laden Web of Terror

By BENJAMIN WEISER

Federal prosecutors, in a series of little-noticed court filings, have painted the most detailed picture yet of how Osama bin Laden directed what they depict as a worldwide terrorism conspiracy.

The papers filed in the case show an organization that used international companies and a relief organization as cover for its operations; obtained blank passports from the government of Sudan; recruited a network of people living in the United States; and communicated by fax, satellite phone and coded letters, often using not-so-veiled language.

In one letter between group members, for instance, prosecutors say Mr. bin Laden — the exiled Saudi financier implicated in 1998 bombings of two American embassies in East Africa — was repeatedly referred to by the code name "Mr. Sam" or "O'Sam," and the group's members in Kenya were called "the fish people."

When the Federal Bureau of Investigation questioned one bin Laden associate in Texas in 1997, a letter went out warning that the man had been confronted by an "opposition company called Food and Beverage Industry based in the U.S." This, prosecutors said, was a reference to the F.B.I.

"He was given an extensive interview," the letter read. "Give my regards to Sam and tell him to take extra precautions cause business competition is very fierce."

The government has been investigating Mr. bin Laden's operations for nearly five years and has charged him and 16 other people with conspiring to attack Americans, specifically in the embassy bombings in Tanzania and Kenya, which left more than 200 dead and thousands injured.

Mr. bin Laden, who is said to be living in Afghanistan, remains a nebulous figure. Until now, authorities have disclosed only snippets from the reams of documents seized from his associates by investigators, and it remains hazy how much control he has over them and other followers around the world. The indictments of Mr. bin Laden have offered few details about his organization or his direct role in acts of terrorism with which he has been charged.

But prosecutors were forced to show their hand recently, when lawyers for one of the defendants, Wadih el-Hage, challenged the government's assertion that he was dangerous or likely to flee the country.

Mr. el-Hage was arrested in 1998, a year after the Kenyan police, accompanied by American investigators, raided his Nairobi home and seized his personal papers and computer. American authorities tied him to the terrorist conspiracy, and he has been held without bail ever since under stringent restrictions. He has been barred from talking or writing to virtually anyone but his immediate family and lawyers.

Responding to pleas for bail from Mr. el- Hage's lawyers, prosecutors disclosed evidence in the Federal District Court in Manhattan that

Continued on Page 4

Iowa, 'Polled to Death,' Is Set for Real Thing

Paul Hosefros/The New York Times

Vice President Al Gore and his wife, Tipper, signed "Grandmas for Gore" T-shirts yesterday at a campaign stop in Fort Dodge, Iowa.

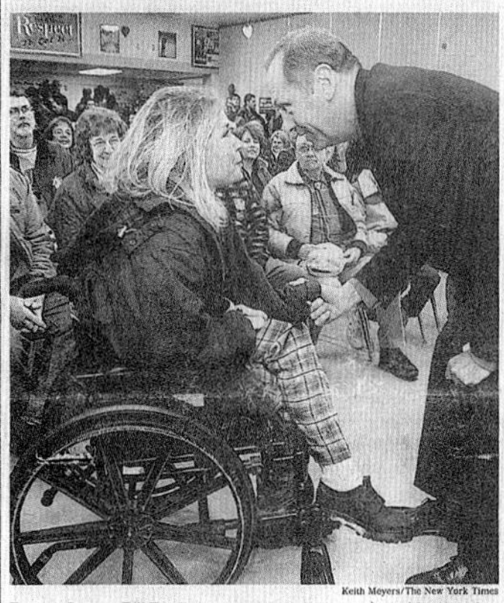

Keith Meyers/The New York Times

Former Senator Bill Bradley went one-on-one yesterday with a member of the audience during a campaign stop at a school in Maquoketa, Iowa.

By RICHARD L. BERKE

DES MOINES, Jan. 22 — Seven presidential contenders scattered across the flatlands of Iowa today in a chase for the unsure and the uncommitted before voters finally have their say in this state's precinct caucuses on Monday, the first crucial test of the 2000 primary season.

The outcome will wound some candidates, embolden others and set the expectations for the nation's first primary, in New Hampshire, just eight days later.

Since polls have consistently found that Gov. George W. Bush of Texas and Vice President Al Gore are widely favored in their parties' voting here, the question among strategists has been just how much support they can attract. Despite the confidence of prognosticators, however, polls in this state are notoriously unreliable because it is difficult to identify caucus-goers. The judgment day that counts, of course, is Monday.

This is the first time since 1988 that both parties have had spirited contests here. Buoyed by the support of unions and the state's top elected Democrats, Mr. Gore is trying to pile up a sizable lead over former Senator Bill Bradley of New Jersey, who has made Iowa a priority and pumped more than $2 million in resources here.

Mr. Bush, who also has waged an aggressive drive, is trying to beat back an unflagging challenge from Steve Forbes, the wealthy publisher who has built a vast organization in Iowa. Mr. Bush's supporters also hope that an impressive showing on Monday will help him halt any surge in New Hampshire for Senator John McCain of Arizona. Mr. McCain skipped Iowa and is concentrating on New Hampshire, where he leads Mr. Bush in some surveys.

Three other candidates are battling Mr. Bush and Mr. Forbes, largely for the loyalty of religious conservatives: Alan Keyes, a former State Department official; Gary L. Bauer, who headed a conservative organization; and Senator Orrin G. Hatch of Utah.

"The die is cast," said Steffen Schmidt, a professor of political science at Iowa State University, who noted that poll after poll had found Mr. Gore and Mr. Bush comfortably ahead. "And I think that any dramatic reversal of the way things are would be astonishing. The place has been polled to death."

As they crisscrossed the state today on planes, vans and buses, contenders sought to energize their sup-

Continued on Page 15

Bush's Stand on Abortion

Gov. George W. Bush said he backed the Republican position on abortion, which calls for a constitutional ban on the procedure. Page 14.

FOR MANY STATES, HEALTH CARE BILLS ARE TOP PRIORITY

FOCUS IS ON H.M.O. COSTS

Legislators Across the Nation Say They Cannot Wait for Congress to Take Action

By CAREY GOLDBERG

BOSTON, Jan. 20 — When Massachusetts lawmakers returned to work this month, these jumbo-sized, hard-to-chew items were on their legislative plate: the financial meltdown of the state's biggest health maintenance organization, Harvard Pilgrim Health Care; rising prices for prescription drugs, and the lack of an H.M.O. patients' bill of rights.

And more: the confidentiality of medical records; prompter payment by insurers; long-term care; nursing salaries, and on and on, for at least 400 bills related to health care.

As they contemplated the labor ahead, the Massachusetts legislators could at least console themselves that they were far from alone.

According to the National Conference of State Legislatures, health care issues made up a greater proportion of bills in state legislatures around the country than any other topic in 1999, about 27,000 bills out of about 140,000.

About 1,400 of those health care bills became law last year. Although fewer state legislatures are in session this year — 44 as opposed to 49 — already 16,000 health care proposals, again the largest proportion of 104,000 bills on the table, have carried over or been introduced for 2000. A good percentage will pass, said Lee Dixon, director of the health policy tracking services of the National Conference of State Legislatures.

"There is every likelihood that the states will continue to enact legislation that addresses the concerns of the citizens of the states around access to care, managed care cost of health care," Mr. Dixon said. "It's a populist issue. It's not a republican or Democratic issue. It's state legislators and legislatures trying to address the needs of their constituents."

At a time when Congress is stuck on many critical health care questions, some state lawmakers say they feel as if they are bearing the brunt of the burden, struggling to fill the most gaping holes in the medical system. They cannot wait for Congress, they say, to tighten controls over managed care, to expand health insurance coverage, to begin addressing the rise in demand for long-term care, and more.

While the states can serve as laboratories for what later becomes federal policy, some legislators say the load is feeling awfully heavy.

"As state lawmakers, we recognize that this has fallen to us, but I think you would be hard pressed to find many legislative leaders in the country who don't think the time is ripe for a national health policy of some sort," said State Representative Gerard M. Martineau, the Democratic majority leader of the Rhode Island House. "Some sort of solution is necessary. It's just too big, and we've been doing the best we can."

In Rhode Island, lawmakers have just helped assure the transition of 125,000 patients to new health care plans after Harvard Pilgrim pulled

Continued on Page 18

INSIDE

Family Values, Cuban Style

The grandmothers of Elián González said in an interview the boy belongs in Cuba, where he has a father and a family who love him. PAGE 12

New Russian Commander

Russia replaced a key military commander in its Chechnya effort as it continued to face stiff resistance in the Chechen capital. PAGE 8

Guatemala Arrests

Arrests in the 1998 death of a Guatemalan bishop who accused the military of atrocities followed the president's vow to investigate. PAGE 10

A Jubilee in a Renewed Rome

Pilgrims arriving for the Holy Year will find restored monuments, piazzas reclaimed from autos and a full calendar of spiritual events. TRAVEL

Some Kind of Duchess

Society, politics and fashion in the late 18th century wouldn't have been the same without the star of "Georgiana: Duchess of Devonshire," by Amanda Foreman; reviewed by Patricia T. O'Conner. BOOK REVIEW

Music for the Home

A new, mature black pop is emerging — music for the living room rather than the streets. It just doesn't have a name yet. ARTS & LEISURE

The Vows Unmade

The wedding was put off, but the reception went on, and the "nonbride" was there, in black. PAGE 38

The Re-education of Al Gore

Shaken by the indifference of voters, the candidate discovers that what works for him is politics. MAGAZINE

Eat or Be Eaten for Insurers

As regulatory barriers between insurance, banking and brokerage houses dissolve, the big mutual insurance companies are racing to go public, hoping to acquire smaller rivals before they themselves can be gobbled up. MONEY & BUSINESS

Money in the Middle

To get elected, stay in the center and spend $3 billion. WEEK IN REVIEW

News Summary 2

International 3-11
National 12-20
New York 25
SportsSunday 27-36

Obituaries .... 23-24 Real Estate 39

Updated news: www.nytimes.com

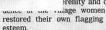

Ecuador Coup Shifts Control To No. 2 Man

By LARRY ROHTER

LIMA, Peru, Jan. 22 — After 18 hours of chaos that began when dissident millitary officers and Indian groups overthrew the elected president of Ecuador, Jamil Mahuad, the country's vice president assumed power early today when a rival military faction intervened on his behalf.

Gustavo Noboa Bejarano took office after Gen. Carlos Mendoza, the Ecuadorean armed forces chief of staff and acting minister of defense, abruptly announced that he was dissolving the three-man junta he briefly led in Latin America's first military overthrow of a sitting civilian president in more than a decade.

General Mendoza said he was acting to "prevent the international isolation of Ecuador," a reference to demands by the United States and Latin American countries that constitutional rule be preserved in a country undergoing severe economic crisis.

"Under the laws laid out in the Constitution, I find myself under the obligation to assume the presidency of Ecuador," Mr. Noboa, who becomes the sixth chief of state in four years, said this morning at a news conference in Quito, the capital. "I have the support of the armed forces and the national police."

Mr. Naboa's assumption of power was formally ratified by the Ecuadorean Congress in Guayaquil today.

Mr. Mahuad, a 50-year-old former mayor of Quito, left the Presidential

Continued on Page 11

Fire, Prayer and a Loss of Innocence at Seton Hall

By DAN BARRY and ANDREW JACOBS

With broken bits of prayer they begged God to save them as the smoke thickened and the orange glow beneath their door brightened. The three young women, cowering against their college room's window, then sought comfort in a trembling recitation of that most familiar of Christian prayers, the Lord's Prayer.

But no rescuers came for Alyssa Merla and her two roommates. Seeing no other choice, they breathed in the tainted air, reached for one another's hands and dashed into the eye-stinging blackness. Somehow they made it down the stairs and emerged into the 10-degree cold outside, their knees bruised from crawling, their faces streaked with soot and tears. Ms. Merla was wearing pajama bottoms and a T-shirt with the name of her school: Seton Hall University.

Ms. Merla was hospitalized for a day for smoke inhalation. But she would soon learn that she had been among the fortunate in the brief fire early Wednesday in a third-floor lounge of Boland Hall, the freshman dormitory at Seton Hall. Three freshmen were killed, including one of her best friends. Another friend was among five students seriously burned; at least three remain on ventilators at nearby hospitals.

Ms. Merla is 18 years old, a physical therapy major from West Long Branch, N.J., with long brown hair and a face that seems incapable of hiding emotion. But a flash point in time has aged her, she acknowledges. "Life will never be the same."

So too has Seton Hall University been transformed. Its history as a venerable Roman Catholic institution of 10,000 students, nestled in peaceful South Orange, N.J., will now

Continued on Page 25

Terry Logan

The January 2000 page of the Rylstone Women's Institute calendar, which has captivated Britain.

The Stately 'Calendar Girls' Dressed So Simply in Pearls

By WARREN HOGE

Rylstone Journal

RYLSTONE, England — It would hardly occur to someone looking for exhibitionists to come to the Yorkshire Dales village of Rylstone, a picture perfect collection of cottages and a duck pond on the road between Skipton and Kettlewell. Much less would someone seek them out among the sisterhood of the Women's Institute, a wholesome rural service organization known for "jam and Jerusalem" — the home bottled preserves from English country kitchens and the Blake poem enshrining "England's green and pleasant land."

So it provoked some wide-eyed interest when word went forth from this pastoral place that 11 members of the Rylstone and District chapter of the Women's Institute, ages 45 to 66, had decided to substitute the usual images of watery sunsets and hiking paths bursting with buttercups on their annual calendar with pictures of themselves with no clothes on.

But what proved even more surprising than the event was the response to it.

The women had come up with the attention-getting notion as a way of raising money for leukemia research, a mission that took on a poignant urgency after the husband of one of their members died of the illness. They hoped that by the deadline of their campaign sales of the $8 calendar might reach $2,000. They reached $550,000.

In another unexpected reaction, their calendar, a discreet and tasteful sendup of the garage mechanic model, brought forth thousands of letters from middle-age women saying that the serenity and confidence of the village women had restored their own flagging self-esteem.

"We're in our 50's, and it doesn't

Continued on Page 10

american adventure

'We were really made into celebrities in America … people stopped us in the street to say "Well done".'

Angela Baker

On Sunday the 23rd January 2000 the *New York Times* carried Warren Hoge's story on its front page, under the headline 'The stately "Calendar Girls", Dressed so Simply in Pearls'. The effect was immediate.

'On Sunday evening I had a phone call at home from a Hollywood director's finder,' says Matthew Baker. 'He explained that he had read the story, and wanted to get on a plane tomorrow and come out and see us, and was asking for directions to the house. I said "Hold on, we're already talking to a production company", and he asked "Is it Working Title? I don't think you should be talking to them. Give me your email address and we'll talk tomorrow. It will be so good to see you".'

For Harbour Pictures the timing was as bad as it could be, according to producer Nick Barton. 'Suzanne and I were at Sundance (the annual film festival founded by Robert Redford and held in Utah) and in negotiation with Buena Vista when the story broke in the *New York Times*.

'We were worried there would be a lot of approaches from American studios because, although we'd been in negotiation with the Girls, they hadn't actually signed the contract with us at this stage. Buena Vista were concerned there would be American producers all over the Yorkshire Dales, and we were concerned because we'd commissioned the script already.'

The publicity also stimulated a completely unexpected demand – there were 60,000 orders that weekend alone for a calendar that had just sold out. Hoge had mistakenly included a website address for an internet company based in the nearby village of Bordley, which ended up getting 200 hits a minute through its email.

'Buena Vista were concerned there would be American producers all over the Yorkshire Dales.'

Nick Barton

'I'd always wondered why America hadn't taken any interest, because I just thought it was something they would love.' *Angela Baker*

The coverage was self-perpetuating, as the UK press started to cover the story of the calendar being taken up by America and the American media flocked to get their own version of the story. *People* magazine sent its own photographer and reporter over to Cracoe, managing a first in its way – a nude picture of Terry Logan apparently being painted by his fully-clothed wife.

Angela believes there is something more than fate involved in the timing of this. 'I'd always wondered why America hadn't taken any interest, because I thought it was something they would love and we had always received letters from America. Now I know why. It's a good job America didn't find us at the same time as England, because we learnt so much here about selling and distributing the calendars, and how to cope with the media. We were all a bit wiser. If it had all come at once, I believe it would have been too much. I just think that John sorted that out for us.'

Meanwhile, the team were off to London to do the shoot for the billboard to promote what turned out to be a washing powder, Surf, or Scurf as Beryl dubbed it. After spending a night at a London hotel, ten of the team were collected and taken to the studio where an all-female crew directed the photography to the sound of Abba's greatest hits. The shots eventually ended up on billboards in London, Manchester and Glasgow. They showed the women in two rows, the ones at the back holding sunflowers while the front row arranged their

limbs to protect their modesty. In the foreground is a single packet of washing powder and over their heads the legend 'We'd rather go naked than go without Sun Fresh'. Eventually the billboards became a familiar sight, though Beryl says when she first saw the posters, 'I was awestruck. We were in a taxi and I just wanted to crawl under the seats.' But later they decided to have their photograph taken next to the billboard in Manchester. 'We were pointing up at ourselves,' says Ros, 'and the traffic came to a standstill. They were all hooting at us.'

And still the US media attention continued, as the NBC television network sent out cameramen and a senior correspondent, and ABC decided to devote a whole programme of the *20/20* show to the story of the calendar. The producer Ene Riisna flew over and established her headquarters in the region's most expensive hotel and then brought a team of eight over for the filming (the BBC had made do with just two). The crew followed them all around the Dales, with repeated shots of them

The billboard advertisement that made Beryl want to crawl under the seat of her taxi.

American TV crews set up camp inside (and outside, *right*) the Logans' house.

walking through fields with sheep, sitting in kitchens and living rooms and, of course, attending a WI meeting that was specially staged for the occasion.

Ene Riisna proved to be a valuable contact, putting the Calendar Girls and Terry Logan in contact with an agent in Canada, who then found them a US publisher, Workman, to produce a calendar for the American market. It was plain that demand would be far too much for the existing team to have coped with this extra work. As it was, Terry dealt with all the practicalities on the printing side, while Tricia put together the background material: press cuttings, letters and brief biographies of all the women involved. This also gave the calendar a second lease of life in Britain, as Terry explains:

'They used the same photographs but changed the graphics to suit the US market. At the same time we told them that there was still a lot of interest in it in this country, so they decided to appoint a printer over here. They sent over the printing plates and had it produced in this country as an eighteen-month calendar. So it had a second life here for another year with American graphics on it.'

The calendar team decided to share the royalties from the calendar between the Leukaemia Research Fund and its equivalent in the United States.

The eighteen-month calendar produced by Workman started in June 2000 – eerily, on the day of John's birthday – and went right through to December 2001. This got calendars into the shops to make the most of the publicity and in time for

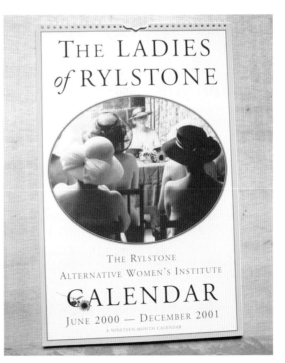

The American version of the calendar.

Nick Barton, Helen Mirren, Angela and Suzanne Mackie being photographed by Tricia.

Angela was torn between being loyal to Harbour Pictures and being fair.

America's Mother's Day. The new format meant using extra photographs, but Terry was able to supply out-takes from the original shoots.

Angela, Tricia and Beryl were chosen to go on a promotional tour of the US to speak at bookstores and to do interviews on television and radio. But, by this time, the issue of the film – should there be one and, if so, who should produce it? – was dominating the team's discussions, and it was producing dissent. Several papers had run stories in March putting forward the possibility of Hollywood remaking the story using American stars. 'Will Julia Roberts strip for the WI?' asked the *Express*, while the *Telegraph* reported that 'Hollywood moves in on the WI pin-ups'. Meanwhile Victoria Wood, a writer and performer especially loved and famed for her portrayal of Northern womanhood, had also become interested in writing and producing a

film about the calendar after contacting one of the girls. Angela was torn between loyalty to Harbour Pictures and being fair to the competition. She felt that it would be cruel to just rebuff Victoria Wood and thought they should 'at least hear her ideas and see what she had to say'.

For Harbour Pictures, this was a very big setback. 'Victoria Wood is national treasure. How could we possibly compete with that?' Suzanne Mackie says. 'It didn't reflect well on us as a company with Buena Vista. We kept saying that we had the women's word, but we had nothing on paper.'

One problem was that while Victoria Wood had been in the national spotlight for more than twenty years since she was a first-year drama student at Birmingham University, neither Nick Barton nor Suzanne had any public profile. Suzanne had joined the BBC from drama college as secretary to the deputy head of drama serials. Under producer Michael Wearing, the department was making some of the BBC's best-ever drama, such as *Pride and Prejudice*, *The Buddah of Suburbia*, *Our Friends in the North*.

It was Nick Barton's then partner, Linda Agran, who then offered Suzanne a job as a development producer. When Linda gave it all up to move to Gloucestershire with her husband in 1998, Mackie became Barton's producing partner. Over a long career, Barton had produced commercials for photographer Terry Donovan as well as television documentaries and dramas with Agran, notably Jack Rosenthal's *Bye Bye Baby* and Nigel Williams's *The Wimbledon Poisoner*. But he had never made a film.

'It was very frustrating because a lot of what we do is based on trust. You have a faith and you have to follow your gut instinct,' says Suzanne. 'We had invested a lot in time and money, and would have been liable for massive legal fees, so it was pretty irksome to have someone coming along trying to buy it from under your feet.'

In the end, both prospective film-makers met the Calendar Girls and the Baker family. Matthew says there were several factors in favour of Harbour Pictures, such as the backing that Disney would be able to give the film and its distribution power. A film made with them would be shown throughout the world. When Victoria Wood came to talk to them, they felt she could not really match their offer.

Wood's agent, Phil McIntyre, sent all the women involved two more offers, each offering far more money upfront. For two weeks, tensions ran high.

'We asked her how she would distribute the film and she explained that she would fund it herself, which wasn't very inspiring. It seemed as if

'It was Tricia and Angela saying, "Never mind the lawyers, we love you. Can we meet for a cup of tea?".'   *Suzanne Mackie*

she'd write it and we'd have very little to do with it,' Matthew recalls. 'We went back to my mum's and told her: "It's fantastic that you're here in the room and it's very flattering that you're interested, but we're not in the business of gazumping people who have already done a lot of work". She accepted that, and we parted on good terms.'

But it did not end there. Wood's agent, Phil McIntyre, sent all the women involved two more offers, each offering far more money upfront. For two weeks, tensions ran high. The media lawyers who had been appointed, at Harbour Pictures' expense, to represent the Calendar Girls instructed the two producers not to contact any of them until their decision had been made. In the end, though, the Baker family, Terry and the six key figures signed with Harbour Pictures, including Tricia (played by Helen Mirren in the film) and Angela (played by Julie Walters).

'I was in the Buena Vista office at the worst moment of my career, and it looked as though we'd lose the project, when my mobile rang,' Suzanne remembers. 'It was Tricia and Angela at King's Cross saying, "Never mind the lawyers, we love you. Can we meet for a cup of tea?" We all piled into a car and took them out for tea, at the end of which they said "It was always going to be you".'

Meanwhile, the girls' American adventure was about to take off in every possible way. Suzanne comments: 'At that time we had no intentions for our Calendar Girls characters to go to America.

'Oh my God, we're going to Hollywood!'

We thought that we would take the notion of ordinary people who become overnight celebrities and what might happen to them afterwards. We would show how an ordinary, middle-aged, middle-class life could suddenly be transported by a mad celebrity adventure. That's very much the drama, if you like, even before the trip to America. But the fact they went to the States seemed so excessive, in the nicest possible way, it was irresistible not to use that. It seemed to exemplify the journey that they took.'

Just before the three (Angela, Tricia and Beryl) were about to fly out to promote the calendar, they found that Lynda would be joining them, as the guest of the Jay Leno show *Tonight*. Apparently they had a particular wish to have Prince Charles' favourite Calendar Girl on the show, so Lynda coolly negotiated that she should arrive in California a day before the show, 'to recover from jetlag', so she would be there for two days before the others joined her.

The tour was a hectic, coast-to-coast whirl of book signings, television appearances and radio interviews, interspersed with restaurant dinners with the American publishers and, more importantly, representatives of the Leukaemia and Lymphoma Society of America. In New York, while appearing on the *Rosie O'Donnell Show*, the girls encountered a strange example of American primness. The calendar appeared with a pink Post-it note over Miss October's nipple and they were also told not to say the word. But Rosie made them all say the word in unison, pointing out that the previous week she had been discussing *The Vagina Monologues*. Tricia comments: 'Kids can see the most horrifying stuff on TV all day and night, but they couldn't see our nipples on the calendar.'

The schedule was so crowded that one day started at 4am to allow for regional television companies to record their own interviews via satellite, enabling the trio to cover the US from Chicago to Little Rock, Arkansas.

Angela noticed that there was a very different attitude in America, a sort of instant fame that they had not encountered in Britain.

'We were really made into celebrities in America. Britain is really good at building you up but, when you walk down the streets, people may know who we are but they won't say anything. But in the States, after we'd been on the telly on the *Rosie O'Donnell Show*, people stopped us in the street to say things such as "Well done". In America you are made to think that you are somebody, much more so than in England.'

And so off to Los Angeles and the Beverley Hills Hilton, where Lynda had been relaxing. After a couple of radio interviews over the telephone, they went to the Disney studios to meet some of the top

Tricia, Beryl, Jay Leno, Angela and Lynda

'[Jay Leno] came to see us in our dressing rooms in just his jeans and T-shirt and talked to us. He was lovely. It was only later that we realised how important his show was.'

Angela Baker

executives over lunch, which was served on Mickey Mouse crockery, and then to the NBC studios to record the *Tonight* show with Jay Leno. This was the highlight for Angela.

'It was brilliant. It was his fiftieth birthday. He had a team of 150 people working for him in the studio, and they made him a huge birthday cake with all these candles. Everyone sang "Happy Birthday" and he asked the ladies of Rylstone to come down and get the first slice,' she recalls. 'We had a dressing room with a star and all our names on the door. He came to see us in just his jeans and a T-shirt and talked to us. He was lovely. It was only later that we realised how important his show was.'

From there they flew to San José and drove to Santa Cruz where, after the bookshop sold 250 copies in just half an hour, it had to close because it could not cope with the numbers.

And then back to Britain, where yet another US television company, CBS, wanted to make their own documentary about the calendar. Within weeks the camera crew were filming a WI meeting where the talk was on 'emancipated women's clothes' and Tricia's new Pilates class, as well as interviewing the Girls. Although they had never heard of the *60 Minutes* programme before, the Girls realised that it was a tremendous coup for

Star treatment. Lynda and Tricia outside their own dressing room on Jay Leno's *Tonight* show.

the US version of the calendar as it is transmitted to twelve million homes. An even bigger boost was that CBS postponed broadcasting the programme until the Girls were back in the US in November to promote the calendar in its second US incarnation, in a normal twelve-month format.

On this trip it was to be Tricia, Angela and, appropriately enough, Miss November, Ros Fawcett. It was a gruelling ten-city, fourteen-day tour, though Ros returned after the first week.

The trip started well, as Angela had become accomplished at charming airline staff into upgrading their tickets.

'I was so excited when we got upgraded. We wanted to open the envelope with the tickets there and then, but we couldn't. So we walked round the corner, saw what they had given us and then jumped around. It was the best thing ever. I saw a man with a clipboard and thought he was the one to ask. I waited for my moment, and then went up and said: "You look like a very important man. I wonder if I can ask you a question: can we be upgraded?" And we were. It makes such a difference, going business or first class. It will be very hard to go back to steerage.'

'It was bloody champion' was Tricia's view. This was echoed by Ros. 'We had the goody bags emptied, socks on, masks ready for bedtime, face cream on and everything. We were trying out the fancy leather seats and we were sipping champagne. Angela had a new camera and we took pictures of each other, but she was so busy getting goody bags for everybody that she left the camera on the plane.'

Real life and fiction. Not much difference.

Lynda and Beryl looking cramped and irritable in their barely-big-enough limousine.

And so the Calendar Girls began their tour, wondering when the much-famed *60 Minutes* programme was to be broadcast. It was while they were being driven to Philadelphia they realised that the programme was on that night, but they were not sure if they would feature on it.

Ros says: 'We ended up in a place called Allentown, a real one-horse town in Pennsylvania. We were looking all over for somewhere to watch it, first a supermarket then a restaurant. Eventually we saw this sports bar, and the young girl who was driving us went in to see if they'd let us watch it there. She asked this young barman: "I've got some ladies with me and they've done this nude calendar which is on the *60 Minutes* programme. Can they come in and watch?". The guy asked: "How long's that on for?" I think they expected fabulous models walking in. Instead they got us, all dressed in black and wearing sunflowers. The barman looked at us and just said "a pin-up calendar?".

The television exposure certainly helped. One bookshop that had only sold 350 the week before the show went out then sold 450 a day afterwards. For Ros the US trip had some strange moments, such as when they were just about to finish at a book signing at Madison.

One bookshop that had only sold 350 the week before the show went out then sold 450 a day afterwards.

'The door was flung open and this girl burst in, saying "Thank goodness, I thought I was going to miss you, but I couldn't get here sooner because my car was torched in the car park". The owner had just been telling us how lovely and safe it was living in Madison.'

Nor did her exposure to back-to-back television

interviews while in New York impress her. 'They all blend into one after a while because the ladies on American TV all look the same: hair straightened, perfect complexion, beautiful teeth. They're all coiffured and absolutely spot-on.'

But the publicity worked. That year the Rylstone Ladies were the calendar girls of the US, as its sales of 202,000 copies in the US easily beat rival offerings produced by Britney Spears and Cindy Crawford. Rylstone Ladies' calendar even outsold the celebrated *Sport Illustrated* swimwear calendar, a locker-room favourite for years.

But the year had one last surprise in store: an invitation to appear on stage at the Royal Variety Show together with Richard Stilgoe and Peter Skellern. The duo had written a comic song about the calendar called 'Hi, we are the WI', and the organisers wanted the Girls to accompany them. Ros had originally contacted Skellern and Stilgoe when she heard the song on the radio and ended up arranging all the details. The idea was that the ladies would appear to be naked behind very large songsheets for *Jerusalem*, the WI anthem, during the very last verse of the song. This adapted the words of William Blake's hymn, so that after the line 'Bring me my arrows of desire', the song proceeded to the women singing 'Smear myself in homemade jam'.

Ros had to send down every conceivable measurement (bra size, below bust, above bust, hips, waist, leg length and shoe size), so she thought the costumes would be individually tailored. 'Anybody could have worn them. They were just elasticated pink shifts, like old-fashioned knickers,' says Ros. 'The songsheets were held up with the same sort of copper tubing that plumbers use, while we wore black hats and shoes. We were all wired up with microphones, except for Tricia because she can't sing.'

The team found the whole enterprise a giggle, from having to share their dressing room with what they describe as the 'fit young lads' from Cirque du Soleil to being in make-up at half past nine in the morning so the stars could be made up nearer the time of the performance. After the show they found themselves rubbing shoulders with Shirley Bassey, Lionel Richie, Bryn Terfel and Ben Elton as they waited for Prince Charles to come backstage for the traditional chat.

Christine found herself next to Kylie Minogue. 'She was tiny and birdlike, and very chatty actually,' she says, while the Irish boyband Westlife were 'just a bunch of daft lads, and good fun'.

This was the swansong for the Calendar Girls in their original team. When they returned to Cracoe, they held a meeting at which the five who had not signed up to the film decided they did not want there to be any further calendars, even though Workman had 50,000 advance orders for a 2002 edition. Their photographs and negatives from the original photo-shoot were then destroyed.

The six who remained developed a follow-up: 'Baker's Half Dozen', a shot of them all in similarly saucy poses at Miss July's kitchen table, which would be sold at their talks to raise money for Leukaemia Research Fund.

the film

'Because it's a real story, we all wanted to remain true to its spirit. But we also wanted to make a good film, so we knew we had to take some liberties.'

Nick Barton

Creating a film is a very lengthy process so, while the Calendar Girls were touring America, the script was written, rewritten and then revised several times more. Suzanne Mackie explains: 'It looks effortless. You just copy what is happening. But it's not that simple. Events were unfolding as we were writing the script. To make the story stand up dramatically we invented a lot more, but as the year went by we didn't have to. It took at least twenty drafts to get the script right.'

In Nick Barton's opinion this was crucial and one of the main reasons for going with a wealthy US backer, who could afford to put in the resources at the beginning to prepare the script. He believes that a lot of British movies fail to work because they are under-resourced from the start.

'The majority of British films that have been successes have had American money in them because the US distributors are the biggest in the world, so films like *The Full Monty*, *Billy Elliott*, *Bridget Jones* and *Notting Hill* are all US-backed.

The Full Monty didn't have any British money in it at all,' he points out.

The promise that Nick and Suzanne had made was that the film would be one that would make all involved proud and that the Girls would see the scripts as they evolved.

Angela says: 'At every stage they brought the script to us for our comments and they took our input on board. We were glad we took the decision

Tricia, Helen and Angela on set.

to go with them, because they were listening to us.'

The producers were also adamant that not only would the cast be British but also that the film would be set in Yorkshire. Nick says: 'We wanted Yorkshire to be one of the characters in the film, so that the landscape becomes an integral part of the film. We were very aware that the ladies lived in this fantastic part of the Yorkshire Dales and we felt that it did inform them. If they had come from anywhere else, they might not have done the calendar. So it's been very irritating for us that some people think that we painted in those "picture postcard" shots of the Yorkshire Dales.'

Some commentators even thought that the US tour was included in the film to appease its American backers but, as Suzanne says, 'They went to eleven American cities in real life and we only opted for Los Angeles. They did go on the Jay Leno show and we asked him to do it again. And they did get upgraded on aeroplanes.'

It was in December 2000 that director Nigel Cole joined the project. 'We had a list of several directors, but we knew that Nigel would bring the right sensibilities to the film,' Suzanne says. 'He would allow the comedy to come out of the drama and create a character-led and emotionally layered film: a human story, both funny and poignant.'

Much in demand since his feature-debut, *Saving Grace,* premièred to huge acclaim at the Sundance Film Festival, Nigel chose *Calendar*

The shoot appears to have been a happy experience for everybody: here Ciaran Hinds and John Alderton share a joke off-camera.

Girls over a number of other Hollywood projects in development.

'I like to mix comedy and drama, and *Cold Feet, Saving Grace* and *Calendar Girls* all have that in common. I like making people laugh and cry. I'm a bit of a softie at heart and a little sentimental, but I get embarrassed about that so I like to puncture it with a joke. Romantic comedy is a genre where you can do both,' Nigel explained. 'The fact that this film is inspired by a true story brings its own challenges and pressures. Because it's a real story, we all wanted to remain true to its spirit. But we also wanted to make a good film, so we knew we had to take some liberties.'

Although unfamiliar with the world of the Women's Institute, Nigel found the ladies of Rylstone to be precisely as he had imagined them. 'They are funny and bright, and not at all conservative and dull. These women are in their mid to late fifties, so they were teenagers in the 1960s.

'In the real story, there was very little opposition to what they did. But drama is about conflict, so

'I like making people laugh and cry. I'm a bit of a softie at heart and get a bit sentimental, but I get embarrassed about that so I like to puncture it with a joke.' *Nigel Cole*

Tim Firth and Nigel Cole in a script consult.

The competitive world of the WI cake competition.

'One thing that did surprise me, however, was just how competitive that world is: the WI women take the shows seriously and they really care about winning the prizes.'
Nigel Cole

we had to create some paper tigers, like the board members at the WI conference in London whose approval they need to go ahead, who at first appear horrified by the idea but then come round.

The characters of Chris and Annie were inspired by Tricia and Angela. They were always the naughty ones giggling at the back of the class, so I wanted to reflect that. One thing that did surprise me, however, was just how competitive that world is: the

WI women take the shows seriously and they really care about winning the prizes.'

He was keen to ensure the film wasn't just a knockabout comedy. 'Perhaps, in a different time, the film would have charted the struggle to get the calendar done and would have left the women on a high. I wanted to take it further, because when I met the real women it was clear that, although they were all very happy that they had done this, it wasn't without its tears. I felt that was an interesting part of the story. I wanted to show that they flew quite close to the sun and burnt their wings.

'Also, at the time of working on the script, reality television had just started out and everyone was talking about the first series of *Big Brother*, so we were aware that we were making a film about instant celebrity at the right time. I'm glad that in the last part of the film we addressed the idea of celebrity as a monster that gets out of control.'

Nigel Cole and the actresses discuss one of the fête scenes.

Meanwhile, the film-makers brought on board Tim Firth, the writer of such acclaimed television dramas as *Preston Front* and *Neville's Island*, to rework Juliet Towhidi's screenplay. 'Juliet had created a beautiful and lyrical world for the film,' Suzanne recalls, 'as well as a cast of characters that were fully rounded and completely authentic. But everyone felt that the screenplay needed some additional comic input and a northern voice, which we knew that Tim could provide.'

For his part, Tim was at first a little dubious about the project. He had never been in the position where he had to take over someone else's screenplay and he did not think of himself as a comic writer. 'I can't even tell jokes, let alone write them,' he admits. But the project had an enormous pull on him, as he was extremely familiar with both the story and all the places concerned.

'My Dad is an expatriate Yorkshireman marooned in Cheshire, so we used to holiday in the Dales all the time and spent lots of time in Skipton, Burnsall and Grassington. When the calendar came out, it was a huge novelty for the family. Mum said: "Look, these women are from Cracoe and you've been through it so many times". Before I had any involvement in the film, I had actually bought the calendar from Lynda at Ripley Show the year that it came out. It also turned out that I was on the mailing list for Terry's art gallery, and I'd got five of his paintings in my house.'

Tim's approach was unusual: he did not meet any of the people concerned until he had written a script. He reasoned that this would leave him free to write without making a judgment on their characters and to create a drama that was true to the spirit of the story without being too restricted by the facts.

Fictional account. *Left* the photographer's character changed three times before it was fixed as the hospital porter Lawrence. *Right* Tricia's alter ego Chris has a florist's business rather than an educational medical software company.

'I based a lot of the Chris and Annie characters on the relationship between my mum and her closest friend, who had died recently of cancer. There was a timbre and tone to their relationship that was very truthful and if you listen to how they talk to each other they are like that.

'What's quite hard to grasp if you haven't grown up in this culture is that people define their friendship almost by opposition, by arguing and making jokes at the other's expense. And none of this disturbs the bedrock of the relationship. On the surface you might wonder why these people are friends when they just make fun of each other. They don't throw their arms around each other and declare undying love.'

In the course of writing a drama as opposed to a documentary, a few facts had to be rearranged, as Terry discovered. 'My character totally changed. I was three different characters before I became the hospital porter. I found that rather difficult at first, but they convinced me that it would work better in the script. They said that a former art director

'I based a lot of the Chris and Annie characters on the relationship between my mum and her closest friend, who had died recently of cancer.' *Tim Firth*

living in the Dales wasn't a believable situation. I found that a bit hard to swallow.'

Tricia and Angela had their own difficulties with the script. 'We realised that people would see the film and believe that what happened in it was real. We didn't like the argument between us and the drugs story with the son, but we realised that it had to stay there,' says Tricia, whose business changed from an educational medical software company to a florist's. Angela adds: 'Everybody accepted that reality had to be twisted for the film. The WI didn't get upset at the meetings being portrayed as boring. They just said "Well, some meetings are boring" and left it at that.'

More injections of dramatic fiction. *Above* Gaz and Jem
(Marc Pickering and John-Paul Macleod) in the 'troubled
teenager' storyline.
Below and facing page Marie (Geraldine James) struggling
to maintain 'the unblemished reputation' of Knapeley WI.

By February 2002 the script had got the green
light from Disney and filming was scheduled for
June that year. To provide the necessary authen-
ticity, the film-makers asked the Calendar Girls to
provide a voice tape for the actors so they could get
some sense of the Yorkshire accent. This ruled out
Tricia immediately, as her Sunderland accent is still
instantly recognisable. So Ros, Beryl, Beryl's husband, Terry, Angela and Roy the postman spent
an evening reading extracts from the local paper,
the *Craven Herald*. Their accents grew noticeably
broader as the evening continued. During filming,
Ros found herself the model for Helen Mirren's
accent, as she was the only person concerned who
actually came from that area of North Yorkshire,
having been brought up in Embsay.

In May the notices appealing for extras to appear
in the film were put up all over the Dales, and then
the Girls began to meet their film counterparts.
Tim noted: 'The characters in the film were loosely
based on the real life and had to be inspired on the
spirit of the calendar rather than the detail of it.
But the actresses all sought out the woman whose
character they thought was closest to the role they
played.'

The meeting certainly came as a surprise to the
real Calendar Girls, as Angela recalls: 'We thought
we wouldn't meet any of the stars. Nigel had said
they probably wouldn't want to meet us because
they got our characters from the script. But then I

'The WI didn't get upset at the
meetings being portrayed as
boring. They just said, "Well,
some meetings are boring".'

Angela Baker

'Nigel, what's our motivation?'

had a telephone call that Julie Walters wanted to come and meet me, which was a big starry moment.

I spent two days with John Alderton and that was brilliant. We went on favourite walks that my husband John and I liked, and we talked about John all the time. He went to meet John's staff and the other Calendar Girls of course, my family and grandchildren, just trying to get to know what kind of person he was.' Angela lent him John's watch to wear while filming.

'The great moment for the girls came when they were to play a rival WI group, the High Gill WI, at Kilnsey Show, moved for the occasion to the more picturesque village of Burnsall. The atmosphere was as if it were one big party, as the weather lifted for the whole two days of filming to show the Dales at its most idyllic. There were hundreds of friends and family taking part as extras. (More than 800 locals were recruited to work on the film

in total.) They were all were fed and paid £45 a day to take part. 'The queue to get paid was about three miles long when they finished filming that day,' remembers Ros.

The girls had two trailers to share between them and, after breakfast with the stars, started shooting their scene, which took around five hours. In between takes, Beryl discovered that many of the extras were members of the WI who had been invited especially, so she led them in a rendition of *Jerusalem* between takes, until the director asked her to stop.

More than 800 locals were recruited to work on the film … 'The queue to get paid was about three miles long', remembers Ros.

... 'Pure spite, ladies'

Tim Firth had arranged for his mother, a lifelong member of the WI, to be among the extras and had a little surprise in store for her. 'The prize that the Helen Mirren character wins in the film for the sponge-cake is called the May Wilkinson Trophy. May Wilkinson was my gran and a WI aficionado who died about ten years ago. It was very moving for my mum to hear that name because I didn't tell her

£45 for a job well done. The extras, recruited from the local community, queue for their day's pay.

before, and she now has the trophy in her kitchen.'

Many people who had featured in the real story of the calendar found themselves on film, though only Roy the postman appeared as himself. Terry Logan, for instance, found himself cast as one of the paparazzi. And sometimes life and art became confusingly entangled. The BBC crew that had filmed the documentary turned up to record the *Calendar Girls* film being made. But the crew and director ended up with the cameras being turned on them to portray the media frenzy that followed the launch of the original calendar. Then the actresses teamed up with the real Calendar Girls to produce another calendar, again photographed by Terry Logan, to raise money for Leukaemia Research.

Once the film had been edited ready for release, the girls found themselves swept up by the busy schedule of promotional work that attends any film launch. This ranged from a glamorous première at

Above Terry Logan, dressed for his part in the film as a paparazzo, talking to the production photographer, Jaap Buitendijk.
Below Who's filming whom? A BBC crew arrived to film the filming of the film, but found themselves filmed instead.

the Cannes Film Festival, to the local opening in Skipton for the people who had taken part as extras. The demand for the girls to appear at festivals and premières in Europe was so great that they could only go in twos and threes, leaving them with warm memories of receptions from Stockholm, Hamburg, Vienna, Dinard, Rome and Barcelona.

For Christine, the after-show party in Stockholm was particularly memorable. 'When we came to leave, Helen Mirren went out with the boss of Disney. We were at the back of the table so it took us longer to shuffle out. As we were walking through the long, narrow restaurant, we got one or two people waving and shouting goodbye to us. People started to clap, and the whole place was applauding us as we left. Helen Mirren was standing outside, and she threw her arms around me and said "How cool was that?". The applause hadn't been for her, because she was already outside. It was for us. It brought a tear to the eye.'

Naturally, the première in Los Angeles, the capital of the film industry, stood out, not least because it was attended by Kevin Costner. His movie, *Dances with Wolves*, had been the Bakers' favourite. 'It's the one film I can remember going to as a family with everyone, like a charabanc trip.

'People started to clap, and the whole place was applauding us and we left. Helen Mirren was standing outside, and she threw her arms around me and said "How cool was that?".'

Christine Clancy

Another calendar ... another fan.

He told my mum "Ah'm in awe of you ladies", and he laughed in the right places during the film,' says Matthew.

Not everyone was so in tune with the spirit of the film, Tim Firth observed. 'There were some extraordinary clashes between the North of England spirit and Hollywood attitudes. My favourite was when a woman came over to Angela in LA and introduced another American woman, saying, "This is Angela Baker and she lost her husband to leukaemia and that inspired the film". The other woman gripped Angela's hand and said "Oh congratulations".'

But the climax for all concerned was the charity première at the Leicester Square Odeon. 'It was like a wedding, a funeral and a christening all rolled in together. Every emotion was there that evening. It was awesome in its magnitude,' Terry recalls. Welcomed like film stars, put up at London's top hotels and taken to the cinema by limousine, the Calendar Girls were taken aback by the scale of their red-carpet reception.

'[The première] was like a wedding, a funeral and a christening all rolled into one. Every emotion was there that evening'

Terry Logan

Big in America: film promotion in Hollywood.

'We are so used to ordinary things. We're not used to being treated like celebrities and having to wait to get out on a red carpet,' says Beryl. 'There was a group of women walking past with tickets in their hands and my husband said they looked like WI women. The next minute they all started singing *Jerusalem*. It was just magic.'

Through the film, the Girls and their families relived the events of the past years, the sorrow that started them on their extraordinary journey and the triumphs along the way. Invited on stage afterwards, they were given a standing ovation by the audience. The day was rounded off with a sumptuous dinner for a thousand guests at the Grosvenor House Hotel, where Beryl was treated to a very special chorus of 'Happy Birthday' in honour of her seventieth.

'It was dreamlike, like your wedding day. I love to relive it,' says Ros. Each table was done as a month of the year, with flowers from that season as the centrepiece. The place mats were decorated

'There was a group of women walking past ... and my husband said they looked like WI women. The next minute they all started singing *Jerusalem*. It was just magic.'   *Beryl Bamford*

Calendar Girls real and honorary, including *(standing)* Celia Imrie (second left), Helen Mirren, Julie Walters, Angela Baker, Tricia Stewart, Beryl Bamforth and Ros Fawcett; *(seated, left to right)* Lynda Logan, Annette Crosby, Penelope Wilton, Christine Clancy and Linda Basset.

with photographs of the *Baker's Half Dozen* and the actresses from the film. Ros even spotted some actors taking these as souvenirs.

And so back to Yorkshire, Cracoe and normality. Beryl says, 'Local people help us to keep our feet on the ground. We're here to do a job and we enjoy doing it, and that's it.'

Tricia adds: 'We enjoy things and get excited, but we're not really overwhelmed by anything. We've got used to doing a lot of different things. The calendar is famous, but we aren't film stars.'

Angela has found some parts of the calendar's success quite hard to bear, almost underlining her widowhood. 'You're with all the other women who have husbands, who are excited to see them again. They're meeting up with them and kissing them, which is natural. If John had been here, that's what we'd have been doing. It just feels horrible. But, you have to get on with it.'

She takes strength from a remark made to her by a woman at the Leukaemia and Lymphoma Society of America, New York Chapter. 'I said "It's my dream to make a million", and she replied "Just think, my dear, this could be the million that everyone's waiting for". And wouldn't that be a perfect ending?'

calendar girls country

The countryside featured in the film *Calendar Girls* is among the most beautiful to be found in Britain. The landscape ranges from picturesque villages by tranquil streams to the most rugged and bleak of fells. As is often the case in films though, the places that appear to be quite close on celluloid are many miles apart in reality.

In the film, all the girls in the calendar live in the fictional village of Knapeley. In the film this is represented by the pretty village of Kettlewell, which is about 10 miles from Cracoe, where the girls do live. Kettlewell is also more than twenty miles from the Cow and Calf Rocks at Ilkley, where the emotionally confused Jem retreats to muse upon his mother's strange clothes-shedding behaviour. But, with the exception of Settle, all the locations are within Wharfedale, an area rich in a history that dates right back to the Romans and beyond.

The area now seems sparsely populated but, from the Middle Ages until the early nineteenth century, Wharfedale was part of a web of commercial and industrial networks that spanned the North of England. In the twelfth century feudal lords enabled many monasteries and priories to be founded in the area and endowed them with huge tracts of land. These were cleared of forests to produce the open fells seen today and used to farm sheep, as the wool trade was immensely profitable.

The feudal lords are also, indirectly, responsible for the network of green roads that cross the dale. These date back to when they were granted charters to hold markets in the towns they owned. These became wealthy and were soon linked to other towns and villages by packhorse trails that now survive as green roads. The market roads also led to many of the wooden Wharfedale bridges being rebuilt in stone. Later still, in the seventeenth and eighteenth centuries, these became part of the droving routes along which herds and flocks were driven, first to be fattened in northern England, and then to the southern fairs.

The feature that impresses most newcomers to the dales on first sight is the massive patchwork of drystone walling that snakes over the steepest fell. Some of these do date back to monastic times and some were built just to mark property boundaries or restrict stock from straying and can be recognised for their irregular shapes and crooked walls. But the great majority were built from 1780 to 1820, the era when much of the land throughout England switched from being held in common, so that everyone could farm it, to being held by individuals. In other areas this could be done cheaply, with hedges that could be simply planted. In the dales this was done with the only material available: stone. The walls built for the enclosures are straight, without compromise to any contour or cliff, because they were drawn up on maps that were laid before parliament in Enclosure Acts.

These walls are impressively monumental in scale but, in a sense, grim because they are a visible record of how little a man's labour and life was worth compared to that of a sheep, the only farm animal that could thrive on much of the poor grazing to be found on the uplands. A wall six feet high would contain nearly two tons of stone for every yard and, to be considered a good waller, you had to be able to erect seven yards a day. That meant shifting twelve tons of stone and lifting each stone an average of three feet. All that work just to stop sheep straying.

The buildings of Wharfedale follow a plan first introduced by Angles and Danes long before the Norman conquest. They built houses by forming a bay with a cruck (rather like an A-frame) at each end, and then filling in with whatever material was available. All that was required for more

Drystone walls and barns near Kettlewell.

accommodation, whether for people or cattle, would be another bay. Even when stone became the main material for walls and roofs, the house remained true to this pattern, with a low-pitched, stone-slate roof, mullioned windows and carved and dated lintels above the doors. The mullioned windows are a Tudor fashion adopted rather later by the local masons, and were then often replaced by Georgian sash windows at the front, where the façade was often rebuilt with a central doorway.

These features are particularly prominent at Burnsall, the site of the Kilnsey Show in the film. The village has its own annual event, Burnsall Sports, which includes the oldest fell race of its kind, dating back to around 1850.

The village is next to what was once an important river crossing and has been inhabited since Viking times. The name itself is thought to be Danish in derivation. Restorers found Anglo-Danish crosses built into the walls of the church, which itself dates back to Norman times, though it was rebuilt during Henry VIII's reign.

Next door to the church is a schoolhouse, built at the expense of Sir William Craven in 1602. Sir William is the area's 'Dick Whittington', the local lad who went to London and became the lord mayor. The building is still in use as a school, though it is no longer a grammar school taking boarders but a primary school. Sir William also paid for a bridge to be built and, although it has been rebuilt several times since, it retains the five arches and other features of the original.

Kilnsey itself features in the film because it has the pub, the Tennant Arms, where the husbands sit and drink while the calendar is being photographed, and where Chris and Annie think no-one has

Rylstone Fell.

turned up for the press launch of the calendar. The village is famous for Kilnsey Crag, a massive 170 foot limestone rock face that overhangs by 40 feet. The village was also the site of the grange for Fountains Abbey, housing lay brothers who would administer the monastery's extensive estates in Craven. Thousands of sheep were driven here from all over Wharfedale to be sheared, while the wool would be taken back to Fountains Abbey to be sold all over Britain and the Continent. Kilnsey Old Hall now stands on the site of the medieval grange, which was destroyed after the Dissolution of the Monasteries under Henry VIII.

Rylstone and Cracoe are where most of the Calendar Girls originally lived, though it is replaced by Kettlewell in the film.

Rylstone's other claim to fame is *The White Doe of Rylstone*, a poem by William Wordsworth written after a tour in that area in 1807 when he came across the legend. The story is that Francis, youngest member of the house of Norton in the early sixteenth century, gives his sister Emily a white doe from the moors near their home. Family loyalty takes Francis with his father and brothers to join a rebellion against Elizabeth I despite his premonition of doom. The rebels are defeated and condemned to death. Only Francis is pardoned and he, returning to Norton Tower, is murdered. Emily, coming upon the loyal tenants taking him for burial, sinks down in despair. Out of the forest comes a herd of deer. One of them stops, and lays its head on Emily's lap. It is the white doe, and it becomes Emily's constant companion and comfort in her home in Rylstone, even following her down the valley of Bolton Priory to visit Francis' grave. After Emily dies the doe continues to make the journey, and

Kettlewell, upper Wharfedale.

lies upon the grassy mound under which Emily's brother lies.

Kettlewell acts as the fictional village of Knapely, where Chris, Annie and the rest of the women live.

The village stands where Kettlewell Beck meets the River Wharfe. It appears in the *Domesday Book* as 'Ketelwell' but dates back far beyond. In 1997 workers digging near the village discovered a Dark Age burial site, dating from around 4,000 years ago. The skeleton was of a woman, buried in a crouching position. The village was also the site of the last major battle between the Brigantes and the Roman legions for control of the Yorkshire Dales.

Explanations for the name differ. One authority says it derives from a Norse-Irish chieftain, Ketel, who held the village before the Norman Conquest, while another says its comes from the Anglian *cetel wella* meaning 'a bubbling stream in a deep valley'.

Although the village now looks the epitome of a rural village, it was a centre for both cotton weaving and lead mining right up to the late nineteenth century, with miners moving into the district from as far afield as Derbyshire and Cornwall. There are not many original buildings left unaltered, with most rebuilt in the nineteenth century, though some eighteenth and seventeenth century houses, such as the vicarage, do remain.

Much of *Calendar Girls* was shot in the village or was recreated as an interior in Shepperton Studios. All the scenes of the village hall, for instance, were filmed far south of the Dales, as were the scenes of Chris's house, Annie's house and the photo-shoot at Celia's house.

Other locations can easily be recognised as you walk about the village. For instance the corner café, from which the girls see the camera crews milling

The River Wharfe at Linton.

around when the calendar becomes international news, is actually the village store. Cam Lodge, the scene for John and Annie's house, is on the road behind the Bluebell pub. It is a handsome house dating from the 1860s, with older cottages dating from the seventeenth century nearby. The greenhouse in which John pots his sunflower seeds in the film was built specially and dismantled afterwards.

The footbridge over Kettlewell Beck, where Jem is arrested for smoking what turns out to be oregano, is near the centre of the village. It is likely to date back to the eighteenth century, when it would have also been used by packhorses carrying lead and cotton to market.

The hill where the girls perform t'ai chi in the first and final scenes of the film is behind the village, in a field off Leyburn Road.

Linton has a long and well-deserved reputation as one of the most beautiful villages in Britain, so it is little wonder that the film-makers decided to feature it, making the White Abbey the scene for the photo-shoot and Celia Imrie's house. The name is misleading. It never was an abbey but was built around 1630, as can be seen from the mullioned windows. The house got its name from Halliwell Sutcliffe, a Yorkshire novelist who lived there in the early twentieth century and who set all his books in the surrounding Craven district.

Linton's charm comes from its setting, situated around a green split by a beck which is crossed by stepping stones, fords and three bridges. The buildings are all of local stone so, despite dating from the seventeenth century to the present day and having a variety of architectural features, the various elements of the village fit together harmoniously. Its name probably means 'flax enclosure' (flax was grown

Kettlewell from the fells.

here until 1812) or 'enclosure by the lake'.

The most prominent building is Fountaine Hospital, which was founded and endowed in 1721 'for six poor men and women' in the will of Richard Fountaine. It is said to have been designed by Sir John Vanbrugh, the Restoration dramatist and architect, and is very different from any other building in Wharfedale. The design is quite grand and classical, with a central block comprising of a chapel and an entrance capped by a square tower and cupola, while the almshouses themselves are in wings on either side. The almshouses are maintained from the income from 400 acres of land in Grassington.

To the south of all these villages is Ilkley, which is overlooked by the Cow and Calf Rocks, where Chris's son retreats to get away from the 'weird behaviour' of his mother and her friends.

The town itself can claim to date back to Roman times, when it was called Olicana and had its own Roman fort and garrison, but it only really came to life after the railway was built in the latter half of the nineteenth century. Before this, it was a village by a boggy moor with barely 1,000 inhabitants.

The railway brought the well-to-do merchants of Leeds and Bradford who could then commute to work and, once it had developed a reputation as a spa town, it became a centre for hydrotherapy. At this stage it vied with Harrogate, which was also a famous Northern spa town, to attract visitors to its various hospitals and convalescent homes.

Ilkley Moor is best known as the setting for Yorkshire's national anthem, 'On Ilka Moor Baht 'at' but is also noted for its prehistoric rock carvings, including the Swastika Stone and the Cup and

top A Cracoe backwater.
bottom Burnsall in winter.

top Conistone and Kilnsey Crag.
bottom Cow and Calf rocks, Ilkley.

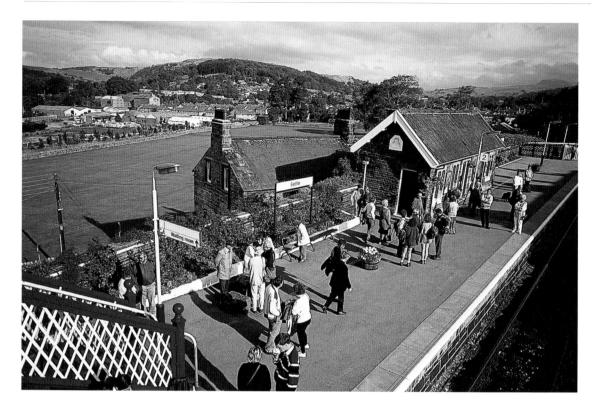

top Settle railway station.
bottom The Leeds-Liverpool Canal as it passes through Skipton.

Ring Stones. The Cow and Calf are on the edge of the moor, huge outcrops of millstone grit from which much of the town was built.

Skipton, the gateway to the Dales, also acts as the setting for the printers and is where the women try to get sponsorship for the calendar. Sheep were an important part of the economy throughout the area, but only Skipton was named after them (the word is Anglo-Saxon for 'Sheeptown').

The town became an important trading centre after the Normans built a castle there soon after the conquest. The castle remains and is one of the most complete and best preserved medieval castles in England, despite being partially destroyed on the orders of Cromwell after resisting Parliamentarian forces for three years during the English Civil War. The Holy Trinity Church next door has a similarly long history, though the present building dates mainly from the early fourteenth century.

Skipton was not simply a rural market town, for the Leeds-Liverpool Canal runs through it. This enabled cotton mills to be built on the sides, as the canal connected it to major ports and markets, and so there are rows and rows of the terraced houses characteristic of the industrial North of England.

Settle is the one town to feature in the film that is not in Wharfedale but in Ribblesdale. It is home to the chemist where Chris goes to pick up her first photographs for the calendar. The town's name is thought to derive from seventh-century Anglian, meaning 'settlement'. It gained importance in the thirteenth century when the lord of the manor won its first market charter from King Henry III.

The town then took shape around the market square, though there are no remains of very early (pre-seventeenth century) houses to confirm this.

In the seventeenth century, Settle was prospering and expanding, and the majority of houses were being built or rebuilt in stone. During this period many of the present houses and inns in Settle were new-built or refronted, some with datestones showing the owners' initials, several with fine patterned carving.

Like Skipton, Settle was also affected by the Industrial Revolution and cotton spinning became the main employment in the town with many mills being converted from corn milling or built for the purpose.

The earliest houses were built with a mix of field-collected water-worn stones (glacial) and locally quarried rubble limestone, rather like a drystone wall. Cut stone was used only for the corner quoins, window and door surrounds. Several of the oldest houses still have the heavy stone flag roof covering and the massive chimney stack that went with them.

Subsequent houses were built with cut sandstone/ gritstone, some in watershot style, which could be neatly layered and mortared, and several of the finer houses were ashlar faced. On these later houses the sandstone roofing slates used were thinner, as new local quarries were opened and techniques improved for splitting the slate taken from them. Much of Settle is now designated as a conservation area, and many of the buildings are Grade II listed.

following page **A panoramic view along Wharfedale towards Starbotton near Kettlewell.**

a brief history of the WI

Despite its very British image the Women's Institute (WI) was founded in Canada in 1897 in the small town of Stoney Creek to provide training and education to women and address the wrongs in predominantly rural society. It has since become a fundamental part of many women's lives throughout the world, offering both mutual support and an important lobbying voice.

Its most famous moment recently came when members gave the Prime Minister, Tony Blair, a slow handclap when he tried to use a platform at their annual general meeting in 2000 to make political points. The WI, a charity, is at pains to be apolitical and heckled when Mr Blair tried to use the occasion to stress his belief in traditional values.

The Calendar Girls were actually at the event in Wembley at the invitation of the then-president, Helen Carey, modelling a fashion show for the three-day event. They missed the slow handclap, choosing instead to miss Mr Blair's speech to have reflexology sessions at £5 a time.

Although depicted in the film as being against the calendar, the WI was in full support throughout. In fact, WI members from all over Yorkshire took part in the film as extras, including Helen Carey.

Although organisations similar to the WI took root in Belgium and Ireland in the first years of the twentieth century, the UK proved more stubborn a convert. The woman who co-founded the WI, Adelaide Hoodless, arrived in Britain in 1899 but her missionary campaigning fell on deaf ears. It was only with the onset of the First World War and the change in the country's economic and social landscape that the war brought that the women of the UK began to recognise the need for the WI.

As the men enlisted, women were needed in virtually every social field. At the Agricultural and Horticultural Union meeting held six months into the war, the discussion turned to the most pressing issue: the need for industrial and agricultural co-operation to meet the national crisis. Madge Watt, a WI member who had come to England to educate her sons, enthralled the audience with an account of agricultural industry in Canada, particularly among women.

The reaction was immediately positive: the agricultural industry began to see the value of women particularly in producing and preserving food, and soon Mrs Watt succeeded in founding the first British WI under the auspices of the Agricultural Organisation Society.

Committed to developing women's talents, the WI now has links with over eight million women in some sixty countries.

picture acknowledgements

This book has been made possible by the unstinting generosity of those in control of our two main picture sources. Buena Vista (UK) International from the very beginning of this project allowed us to use all the shots we needed from their archives, free of charge. Lynda and Terry Logan were not only generous with their own pictures and other relevant items, they spent time explaining the significance of each one and taking further pictures to fill some of the gaps that were left. Many thanks.

The images listed below have all been reproduced with the kind permission of the copyright owners.

©*Buena Vista (UK) International* p.2, p.6, p.12, p.13 (both images), p.14 (top left), p.15 (top right), p.16, p.18, p.19, p.20 (both images), p.21, p.22, p.23, p.24, p.26, p.27, p.28 (top right), p.29, p.30, p.31 (both images), p.32 (main image), p.33 (bottom right), p.34, p.35, p.36, p.37, p.39, p.40, p.44, p.48, p.51, p.52, p.53, p.54, p.58, p.63, p.64, p.74 (both images), p.76, p.77, p.79 (bottom right), p.80, p.83, p.84, p.85, p.86, p.87, p.88 (both images), p.89, p.90, p.91 (both images), p.92 (both images), p.93, p.95 (top), p.96 (bottom left), p.97, p.100, p.101, p.122, p.124 (all images), p.127 (all images).

©*Terry and Lynda Logan* p.9, p.17, p.28 (bottom right), p.32 (bottom left and middle right), p.33 (top right), p.38, p.41, p.42, p.43, p.45, p.47, p.49, p.50, p.55, p.56 (both images), p.57, p.59, p.61 (both images), p.65 (both images), p.66 (both images), p.68, p.72, p.73 (all images), p.78, p.79 (top and bottom left), p.81, p.94, p.95 (bottom left), p.96 (top left), p.98, p.99.

© *Kevin Hopkinson* p.21.

©*New York Times* p.70.

©*Roger Kilvington* p.118-9.

©*Powerstock* p.25.

©*Colin Raw* p.8, p.10 (both images), p.11,
p.14 (top right), p.15 (bottom left), p.46, p.102,
p.104-5, p.106-7, p.108-9, p.110-1, p.112-3, p.114 (top).

©*Bill Wilkinson* p.60, p.67.

Yorkshire Post p.69.

©*Yorkshire Tourist Board (www.yorkshirevisitor.com)*
p.114 (bottom), p.115 (both images), p.116 (both
images).

dedicated to the memory of John Baker